Published in Australia in 2020 by SisterShip Training Pty Ltd

www.sistershiptraining.com

Copyright © SisterShip Training Pty Ltd 2020

All rights reserved. Without limiting the rights under copyright above, no part of this publication may be reproduced, stored in or introduced into a retrieval system, or transmitted in any form or by any means (electronic, mechanical, photocopying, recording, or otherwise), without prior written permission of both the copyright owner/the Publisher.

National Library of Australia data:

SisterShip Training Pty Ltd, 2020, Understanding Weather, The Mariner's Guide

ISBN: 978-0-6451815-0-0

www.sistershiptraining.com

TABLE OF CONTENTS

INTRODUCTION 1
ACKNOWLEDGEMENTS 1
    A Little History 2
    Technology and Advancement 2
THE ATMOSPHERE 3
    What is Weather? 4
    Weather Terms 4
    Atmospheric Pressure / Air Pressure 4
    Barometer 5
    Diurnal Variation 5
    Isobar 6
    Relative Humidity 6
    Backing and Veering 6
    Trade Winds 6
OCEAN CURRENTS 7
CLOUDS 8
    Cloud Classification 8
    Terminology 9
    High Cloud 9
    Cirrus (Ci) 9
    Cirrostratus (Cs) 10
    Cirrocumulus (Cc) 11
    Middle Cloud 11
    Altostratus (As) 11
    Altocumulus (Ac) 12
    Low Cloud 12
    Stratus (St) 13
    Cumulus (Cu) 13
    Stratocumulus (Sc) 14
    Towering Cumulus (Tcu) 14
    Cumulonimbus (Cb) 16
WIND 18
    What is Wind? 19
    Cycles of Air 21
    Air Pressure and Wind 22
BRINGING IT TOGETHER – WEATHER SYSTEMS AND EVENTS 24
    Ridge 24
    Ridge - What does this mean to the sailor? 25
    Depression or Low 25
    Trough 25
    Occluded Fronts 30
    Jet Streams 30
    Jet Streams – What They Mean to Us 31
    Forecasting Frontal Weather 32
    East Coast Lows 32

Katabatic Winds	33
Local Weather Patterns	33
Sea Breeze	33
Land Breeze	34
The Effect of Land and Sea-Breezes on Gradient Wind – What It Means to Us	34
Equatorial Trough/Intertropical Convergence Zone (ITCZ)	35
El Niño La Niña	35
The Indian Ocean Dipole (IOD)	36
Thunderstorms	37
Developing Thunderstorms	37
Tornados and Waterspouts	37
Wind - Apparent & True	37
Wind Vectors	38

TROPICAL REVOLVING STORMS (TRS) OR TROPICAL CYCLONES 39

Development of a Cyclone	39
Warning Signs	39
Three Stages of a Cyclone	40
Tracking a Cyclone	40
Australian areas	40
Cyclone Paths	40
Non-navigable and Navigable Semicircle	40
To Evade a Cyclone	41
Angle of Indraft	42
Storm Surge	43
Measuring the Strength of Tropical Revolving Storms, Cyclones, Hurricanes & Typhoons	43
Saffir-Simpson Scale	43
Australian Scale	43
Cyclone Warning System	44

FORECASTING WEATHER 44

Weather Forecasts	44
When to Listen to Forecasts	44
Sources of Weather Information	44
VHF Broadcasts by State and Territory Authorities	45
Charleville (VMC) Broadcast Schedule	45
WeatherFax	45

READING A SYNOPTIC CHART 46

Synoptic Charts – Mean Sea Level Pressure Analysis (MSLP)	46
Rain or Fine?	50
How Strong Will the Winds Be?	51
Line Squalls	53
Col	54
A Case Study	54
Buys Ballot's Law	56
Forecasting Exercise	56

BUREAU OF METEOROLOGY SERVICES 57

BOM Tropical cyclone services	57
Tropical cyclone seasonal outlook	57
Tropical cyclone outlook	57

Tropical cyclone information bulletin	57
Tropical cyclone watch	57
Tropical cyclone warning	57
Technical bulletin	57
Tropical cyclone forecast track map	57
Tropical cyclone forecast track maps: GIS Compatible Format	58
Marine warnings	58
HF Radio Stations from BOM	59
Notes	60
Notes	62
Telephone Weather Services Directory	62

SUMMARY 65

APPENDIX 1: CYCLONE PREPARATION 66

Anchoring or in a Marina:	66
When a Cyclone Warning is Issued	66
Personal Preparation	67
Detailed Preparation	67
Safety	68
Storm Surge	68

GLOSSARY 69

Introduction

Weather – we can't avoid it.

Good or bad it's always with us but with study and observation we can better prepare and, at times, choose the conditions we'd like to tackle.

It can be a complex subject, so we have provided the basic study of weather from our international commercial and recreational, and teaching experience. These are notes and tips for you to consider during passage planning and when underway; across vast oceans for weeks on end or a day sail across a harbour.

We've incorporated over forty-years combined knowledge while sailing the world. We've sorted through the technical aspects, simplified them, and included what we feel is important to those wandering the oceans and coastlines on boats.

It's a fascinating subject and we hope this helps you better understand that weather forecast adjustments are just one of the many hats mariners wear. Weather forecasts are never going to be perfect, it is our responsibility to interpret, adjust, and prepare.

Acknowledgements

We'd like to thank the Bureau of Meteorology (BOM) and the National Oceanic and Atmospheric Administration (NOAA) for their help and support in allowing us to reproduce some of their information. Particular thanks to BOM, who provided additional information and pointers to help us compile this manual, including pictures/diagrams (Reproduced by permission of Bureau of Meteorology, © 2018 Commonwealth of Australia.)

Huge thanks also to our Editor Belinda Collins and Contributor Viki Moore. Belinda not only transformed this manual to an easy to follow, flowing document but did so with grace and a smile. Viki kindly gave us permission to reproduce her Cloud Article based on her Southern Ocean experiences sailing in New Zealand. We are blessed to call both Belinda and Viki friends.

We've worked hard to reduce any errors but if they do exist they are ours and unintentional. As with all the practical manuals we produce, this is only showing you what we did on board, it is up to you to be responsible for your vessel, crew, and decisions.

Please note:
You can view the pictures contained within this manual on our website. And the links in the book are also listed on our website. Go to www.sistershiptraining.com then select the Weather Course (either via the Courses Tab at the top of the homepage or via the homepage Course Boxes). On the bottom of the page that details the weather course content you will find a direct link to the pictures/links.

What is Meteorology?

Meteorology is the study of weather.

In Greek, *Meteoros* means 'high in the air' and *Logos* means 'discourse'.

As boaters, the weather is an integral part of our life. It dictates our travel and, at times, our destination. Weather is one of the biggest topics of discussion on boats, no matter where you are on Earth, or what type of vessel you have.

Many of us are weather sensitive, that is, our moods are affected by the weather, but once you put some distance between a large land mass, (such as Australia) and your vessel, your mood evens, and sailing the oceans becomes far easier. The weather is often more settled on a daily basis (e.g. no land and sea breeze increasing wind speed) and the sailing and living becomes easier.

A Little History

The first weathermen were high priests, witch doctors, and medicine men. Their job was to predict weather <u>and</u> to modify it with ceremonies, rites and rituals (e.g. calling for rain). Lucky for our forecasters we don't ask that of them!

In the seventeenth century, the barometer and thermometer were invented. This enabled us to actually measure what we experienced.

By the eighteenth century, scientists knew that weather travelled in organised masses of air, for example, weather generally travels west to east. This allowed more reliable communications on weather between locations. Initially townships communicated by smoke signals, then flags (that's how the Sydney suburb Pennant Hills got its name), but this method of communication was slow. In the mid-nineteenth century telegraphic Morse was used.

In the late nineteenth century, Besançon discovered that by sending up a balloon with tiny instruments, he could observe wind and temperature in the upper levels of the atmosphere. We still use this system today. And at the same time, Australia standardised its instruments, weather codes, and telegraph reporting observations.

On the 5th February 1877, the first isobaric pressure map was drawn and published in The Sydney Morning Herald.

The Bureau of Meteorology (BOM) was established in 1908. BOM are Australia's national weather, climate, and water agency. Its expertise and services assist Australians in dealing with the harsh realities of their natural environment, including drought, floods, fires, storms, tsunami, and tropical cyclones. Through regular forecasts, warnings, monitoring, and advice spanning the Australian region and Antarctic territory, the Bureau provides one of the most fundamental and widely used services of government.

Technology and Advancement

Advances in technology enable us to look down on our atmosphere, from space using a network of weather satellites and real time weather monitoring across the globe.

The World Meteorology Organisation manages a program called the World Weather Watch. Established in 1963, the World Weather Watch combines observing systems, telecommunication facilities, and data processing and forecasting centres, to make available meteorological and related environmental information needed to provide efficient weather services in all countries.

Today we can read everyone's interpretations online, whether they are meteorologists on official weather services or the general public on forums; and anyone can access the BOM and study satellite charts. The most assured way to understand weather is to study it. The second way is to become familiar with synoptic and satellite charts and forecast the weather yourself. It is a skill that takes practice. You'll be surprised how quickly your skill develops. Refer back to this manual, ask questions, and predict. Enjoy your boating life safely!

Marine Safety Five Vital Weather Checks
https://www.youtube.com/watch?v=bqp_xSHIbkg&list=PLbKuJrA7Vp7l0EAWKfmE_7jlhjQS07_d3&index=2

The Atmosphere

The atmosphere consists of an ocean of air, extending out to 1,000 km from Earth's surface. All weather processes take place in the lowest 10-15 kilometres of the atmosphere. This is called the troposphere and its upper boundary is called the tropopause. Pressure falls with height, from about 1,000 hPa (hectopascals) at the surface to about 200 hPa at the tropopause. Temperature also generally falls with height throughout the troposphere, at an average rate of about 6°C/km. Because the troposphere is cold at the top and warm at the bottom the air is constantly being turned over as the warm air rises and the cold air sinks (as Highs and Lows). Hence the name troposphere (tropo meaning mixing).

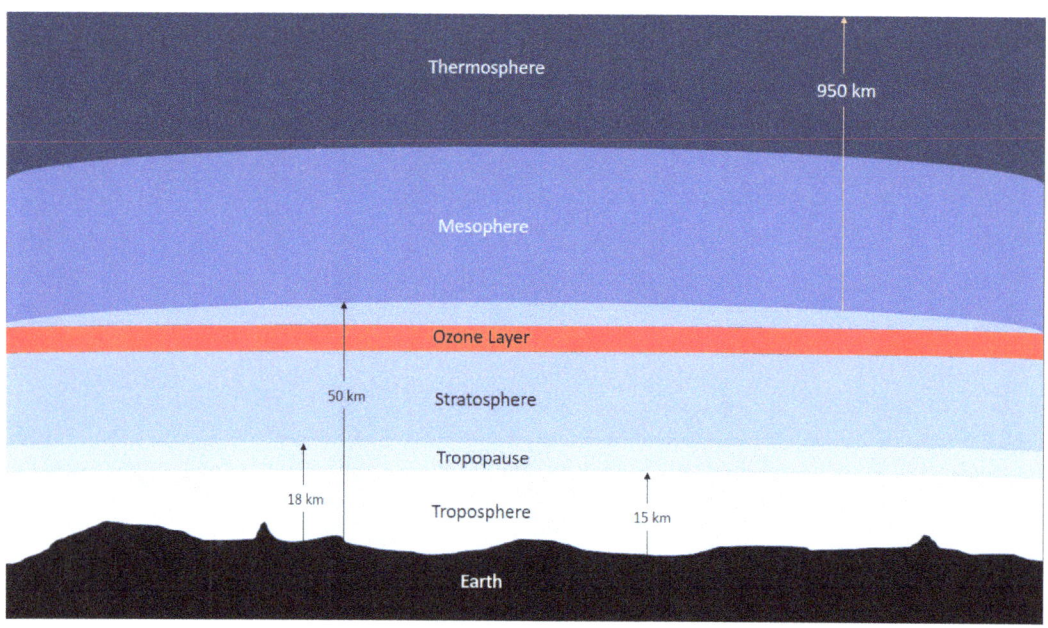

What is Weather?

Weather is the state of the atmosphere at any given time. It's affected by the sun's rays and the ray's interaction with the gases in the Earth's atmosphere. Weather has many aspects, including wind, pressure, cloud cover, temperature, and precipitation.

In the troposphere, the sun's radiation is the source of energy that drives the weather system. There must be a balance between the energy absorbed from the sun and the energy re-radiated into space so that the Earth's temperature doesn't change significantly. The solar energy is spread from the equator towards the poles by our weather systems. Heat and moisture are the two prime causes of weather conditions.

Heat radiation is produced by land mass that heats up and cools down quickly, creating variable wind patterns. This is why large continents, such as Australia, can cause tricky weather for coastal sailing.

Water warms up more slowly than air, but can hold more heat. It takes more energy to increase the temperature of water compared to land. Therefore, the ocean plays an important part in absorbing energy from the sun and preventing the Earth from becoming too hot (and too cold, for example, the Gulf Stream keeps the UK warmer than it would be considering its latitude).

The ocean temperature determines what form the water takes. Mostly the ocean is liquid, but if it becomes cold enough it turns to solid ice. The ocean can become hot enough to pass into the atmosphere as water vapour.

The temperature of the ocean (especially the surface) will vary from location to location and from season to season. The temperature of the ocean is dependent on the amount of solar energy absorbed. The sea retains its heat for longer periods creating a constant temperature over vast areas.

Weather Terms

Atmospheric Pressure / Air Pressure

Air Pressure is the force exerted by the atmosphere on each unit of area. This can simply be thought of as the 'weight' of air. The unit used today (by most nations) is the hectopascal, where 1 hPa equals 100 newtons per square metre. And a millibar (the metric unit for pressure) is one thousandth of a bar (equivalent to 100 pascals).

Barometers measure air pressure in inches of mercury or in millibars. Meteorologists use the millibar measurement and the average pressure at sea level is 1013.25 millibars.

Air pressure changes indicate changes in the weather by high and low pressure systems. These systems determine the weather.

We must pay attention to changes in air pressure.

Barometer

The pressure, and the rate of change of the atmospheric pressure are equally important. To measure changes most boaters use an aneroid barometer (aneroid means movement without fluid). It can respond quickly to small changes but is not as accurate as a mercury barometer. Some aneroid barometers are marked *compensated,* which means that the accuracy of the instrument is not influenced by changes in temperature. If you need to make adjustments for temperature, this is accomplished by adjusting the bi-metal element in the mechanical linkages. The manufacturer will provide instructions on the use of temperature compensation.

The black indicator hand on an aneroid barometer points to the current air pressure. The other hand (usually gold) can be turned to match the current barometric pressure. This makes any changes easy to see. (The black hand moves with a change in air pressure, the gold hand does not). Generally, a change to high pressure means good weather is ahead, and a change to low pressure means bad weather is ahead. In high pressure areas, the air molecules flow to low pressure areas. This is wind.

Your barometer must be located where it cannot suffer shocks or large temperature changes. Keep it out of the sunlight and gently tap before reading to release the built-up frictional resistance.

Diurnal Variation

In addition to changes in pressure due to weather patterns, there is a regular twice daily rise and fall of the barometer. Maxima occur at about 1000 and 2200, and minima at 0400 and 1600. It is caused by the sun heating up a column of air (around noon) which sets a pressure wave in motion that moves around the globe with a twenty-four-hour wave period and a wavelength 180° of longitude. This means that there are two low and two high atmospheric tides each day.

This effect is called the semidiurnal variation of air pressure. This effect, at southern latitudes, is about two or three hectopascals and in tropical latitudes by about five hectopascals. The amount of semidiurnal variation changes slightly during the year.

Always closely monitor the pressure tendency and correct for diurnal variation. When the corrected pressure rises or falls by 6 hPa within a twenty-four-hour period, this will indicate the movement of a high or low pressure system.

You should read/check your barometer at the same time each day.

Storm Type	Pressure (hPa)
Tropical Low	>= 996
Category 1 Tropical Cyclone	986 – 995
Category 2 Tropical Cyclone	971 – 985
Category 3 Tropical Cyclone	956 – 970
Category 4 Tropical Cyclone	930 – 955
Category 5 Tropical Cyclone	<= 929

Isobar

A line on a weather map connecting points which have the same atmospheric pressure at a given time or on average over a given period. It is used to determine the direction and strength of the wind.

Relative Humidity

Humidity is the amount of water vapour present in the air. Relative humidity is a comparison between the quantity of water vapour to how much the air could hold. For example, 50% relative humidity means the air could hold twice as much water vapour as it does at present before it becomes saturated.

A relative humidity measurement of 100% does not necessarily mean that rain is falling. It just means that the air is holding as much moisture as it can at a given temperature, in the form of water vapour, which is an invisible gas.

At near 100% relative humidity, you can still get water vapour condensing into very small water droplets to form clouds, including fog. (The relative humidity at the ground does not have to be 100% to produce rainfall, when this happens it is called *virga*.) Virga is produced when snow or rain is falling from the base of the cloud but evaporates in dry air before reaching the surface.

Backing and Veering

The wind 'backs' when its direction changes in to an anticlockwise direction, for example, from north to west.

The opposite direction, for example, south to west, the wind is said to *veer*, that is a clockwise direction.

Trade Winds

In Australia, the prevailing trade winds along much of the eastern seaboard are southeasterly. They are caused by the movement of air from the subtropical high towards the equatorial low being deflected to the left by Coriolis Force.

Ocean Currents

Temperature and salinity affect the density of water. This results in water moving up or down through the ocean layers and moving as currents around the ocean. As water warms up, the heat makes the molecules spread out and take up space (that is, the water expands), and the density decreases. When water cools, it contracts and therefore becomes denser. This process of heating/expanding and cooling/contracting in the air creates wind.

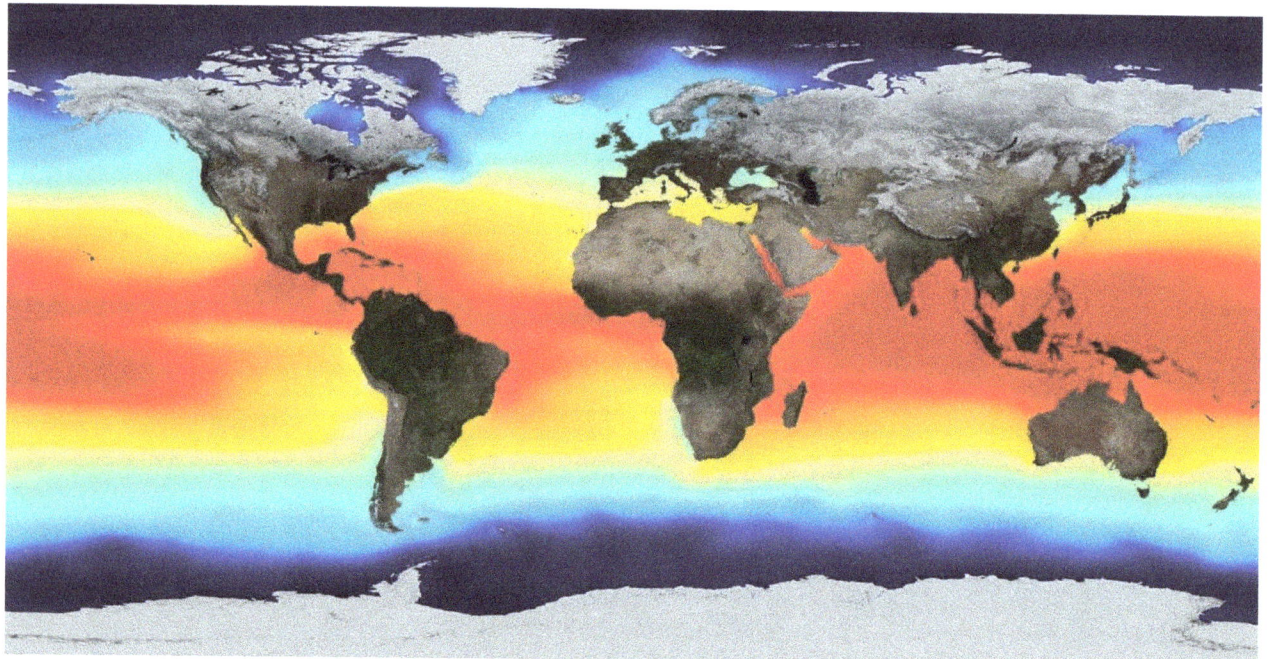

Average Sea Surface Temperature. NASA.

The combination of the sun's heat and evaporation of the sea surface produces the moisture content in the air by way of water vapour.

Water vapour provides the moisture that forms clouds; it eventually returns to Earth in the form of precipitation, and the cycle continues.

> ### A note on currents
> Not only do currents affect a vessel's over-the-ground speed, but a one knot contrary current (to wind) can increase the average wave height by 20%. And two knots can sometimes increase wave heights by 50%.
>
> Opposing currents also produce the kind of steep waves with high, curving backs that can damage even the sturdiest of vessels.

Clouds

Clouds are upper air condensed water vapour. When the upper movement of moist air condenses upon reaching the cooler upper air it condenses into droplets of water (which form around dust or salt particles) forming clouds.

Clouds effect on our weather;
1. Cloud cover will restrict both the heating effect of the sun and the Earth's ability to radiate heat outwards (depending on the density of cloud cover). Therefore, clouds can be the cause of keeping an area cool or warm.

2. Latent heat is released into the atmosphere during the condensation process causing precipitation in the form of rain.

Clouds are identified visually by type of cloud and percentage of sky cover, expressed as *oktas*, for example, one okta (1/8), two oktas (2/8) to 8 oktas (full cloud cover).

Oktas	Definition	Category
0	Sky clear	Fine
1	1/8 of sky covered or less, but not zero	Fine
2	2/8 of sky covered	Fine
3	3/8 of sky covered	Partly Cloudy
4	4/8 of sky covered	Partly Cloudy
5	5/8 of sky covered	Partly Cloudy
6	6/8 of sky covered	Cloudy
7	7/8 of sky covered or more, but not 8/8	Cloudy
8	8/8 of sky completely covered, no breaks	Overcast

The following article on clouds is courtesy of Viki Moore:
https://astrolabesailing.com/2016/09/19/meteorology-clouds/ Published September 2016

Clouds can give big clues about the weather, so it makes sense for sailors to be able to identify the different types of clouds, and what they might mean for the people sailing below them.

While it is easy to focus on what the weather is doing at sea level, clouds give an indication of what is happening above us and provide a three dimensional picture of the movement of the atmosphere.

Clouds show us the stability of the atmosphere, and indicate where we are in a weather system. They can give the first indications of an approaching depression, and indicate future changes in the wind and reduced visibility in rain.

Cloud Classification
Clouds are classified by:
1. Shape
2. Vertical extent
3. Altitude

Terminology
- Cirro — high-Level
- Alto — Mid-Level
- Nimbo/Nimbus — high moisture content
- Cumulus — Heaped or lumpy cloud
- Stratus — Layers of flat cloud
- Cirrus — high wispy

High Cloud
High Cloud is defined as clouds over 17,000ft and above
- Cirrus (Ci)
- Cirrostratus (Cs)
- Cirrocumulus (Cc)

Cirrus (Ci)
Cirrus clouds are the highest and are made up of ice crystals. They indicate the presence of a jet stream and the possible approach of a warm front. No rain.

Cirrus (above) and thick stratus (below).

Cirrostratus (Cs)

These clouds are also made up of ice crystals. As the cloud is very high, it is also very cold, and so the moisture content is low. Cirrostratus clouds are thin and the sun can still be seen – sometimes the sun is refracted, creating a halo around the sun. No rain. (Note: Higher wind conditions can follow the day after the halo around the sun or moon.)

Cirrocumulus (Cc)

This cloud resembles sheep's wool. This cloud is also made up of ice crystals and the low temperature means low moisture. No rain.

Middle Cloud

Middle cloud is defined as clouds around 7,000 – 17,000ft and is called alto
- Altostratus (As)
- Altocumulus (Ac)

Altostratus (As)

Mid-level, featureless grey and overcast layer which extends for many miles. It produces lingering drizzle or light snow.

Altocumulus (Ac)

Mid-level cloud made up of joined or separated cloudlets. This cloud comes in many different formations. As it is lower it is warmer and will have a higher moisture content. Can be ice crystals and water droplets so light rain is possible.

Low Cloud

Low cloud is considered to be from the ground to 7,000ft
- Stratus (St)
- Cumulus (Cu)
- Stratocumulus (Sc)
- Towering Cumulus (Tcu)
- Cumulonimbus (Cb)
- Nimbostratus (Ns)

Stratus (St)

Featureless grey overcast layer cloud – this forms very low and when it is at ground or sea level it is called fog or mist. (Note: May herald a cold front approach.)

Cumulus (Cu)

Fair-weather clouds that form on sunny days. They generally have flat bases and cauliflower-shaped tops. Very light or no rain. (Note: Can herald the approach of a Warm Front.)

Stratocumulus (Sc)

Very common cloud – low layer, individual or joined up clumps or 'cloudlets'. Stratocumulus and Altocumulus look very similar – the only difference is the base of the cloud height. Can produce light showers.

Towering Cumulus (Tcu)

When a normal fair-weather cumulus grows taller than they are wide, then they become Towering Cumulus. They can then form in to cumulonimbus clouds. They can produce heavy showers and have strong up draughts or wind beneath them.

A Towering Cumulus cloud photo from the Bahamas courtesy of Byn Always from <u>Oh Sail Yes blog</u>.

A Towering Cumulus in the Florida Keys (also known as an Anvil cloud) by Jennifer MacLean from <u>Sunshine Coast Adventures</u>.

More Cumulus cloud at Pitcairn Island, Noel Parry in picture. Photo by Jackie Parry

Cumulonimbus (Cb)

This is an enormous storm cloud which has a top shaped like an anvil. This indicates the direction in which the cloud is travelling. These clouds can produce thunderstorms, have heavy showers, and strong winds.

Southerly Front approaching over Lyttleton Harbour New Zealand

Thunder Clouds (Cumulonimbus?) over Lake Macquarie. Photo by Penny Anne Hodgson

Cumulonimbus clouds are one of the few clouds that span the low, middle, and high layers. They resemble the cumulus clouds from which they grow, except they rise into towers with bulging upper portions. Cumulonimbus cloud tops are usually always flattened in the shape of an anvil or plume. Their bottoms are often hazy and dark. There's a nearby threat of severe weather.

Nimbostratus (Ns)
A depressing lingering cloud. It is thick, grey and featureless rain cloud. It is usually formed from thickening and lowering Altostratus clouds. Comes with moderate to heavy widespread rain.

Check out Chris & Wade's photos of clouds on their blog here:
http://sv-takeiteasy.com/2014/07/24/head-in-the-clouds/

Check out Viki's blog, which includes many other meteorology posts:
 https://astrolabesailing.com/

Wind

Wind is a direct result of heat from the sun. The heat causes the warm air to rise and the resulting partial vacuum draws in surrounding air. Upper air which has cooled will fall, this produces surface winds spreading outwards from the point of descent. The sun does not warm up the Earth uniformly and mountains obstruct the wind, therefore the atmosphere is in constant turbulent motion.

Video: https://www.youtube.com/watch?v=9uvMGB3G6X8

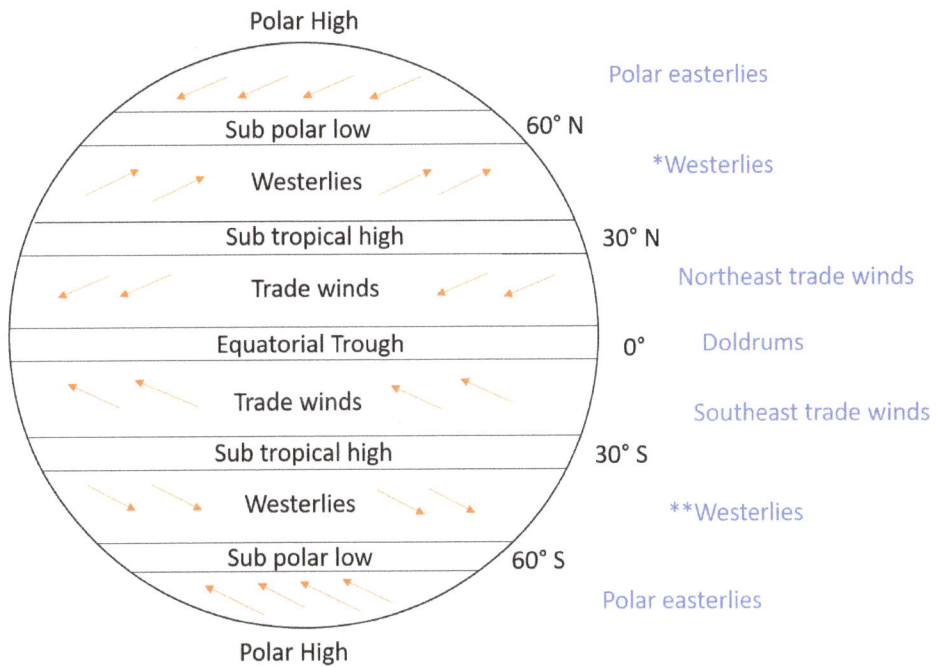

*Close to being westerly wind as the Coriolis effect is larger in higher latitudes
**Wind around the Great Australian bight are more westerly, seeking path of least resistance around the land mass

The diagram above shows the pattern that develops on a rotating Earth.

- The Equatorial Trough has low pressure, light winds, the doldrums
- Trade Winds are northeast in the northern hemisphere and southeast in the southern hemisphere
- Subtropical highs have high pressure, light winds, good weather
- Westerlies blow south of Australia: a succession of cold fronts
- High latitude lows often pass to the south of Australia
- Polar regions have cold, dry, high pressure

Maritime air masses: form over the oceans and Continental Air Masses: form over the land.

There are also: polar maritime, tropical maritime, polar continental and tropical Continental Air Masses.

Trade Winds: prevailing wind directions (see diagrams below under air masses).

Wind blows from high pressure belts to low pressure belts. The spin of the Earth (Coriolis Effect) makes the wind appear deflected on the north–south axis by up to 45 degrees.

What is Wind?

Wind is the movement of gases (air) on a large-scale.

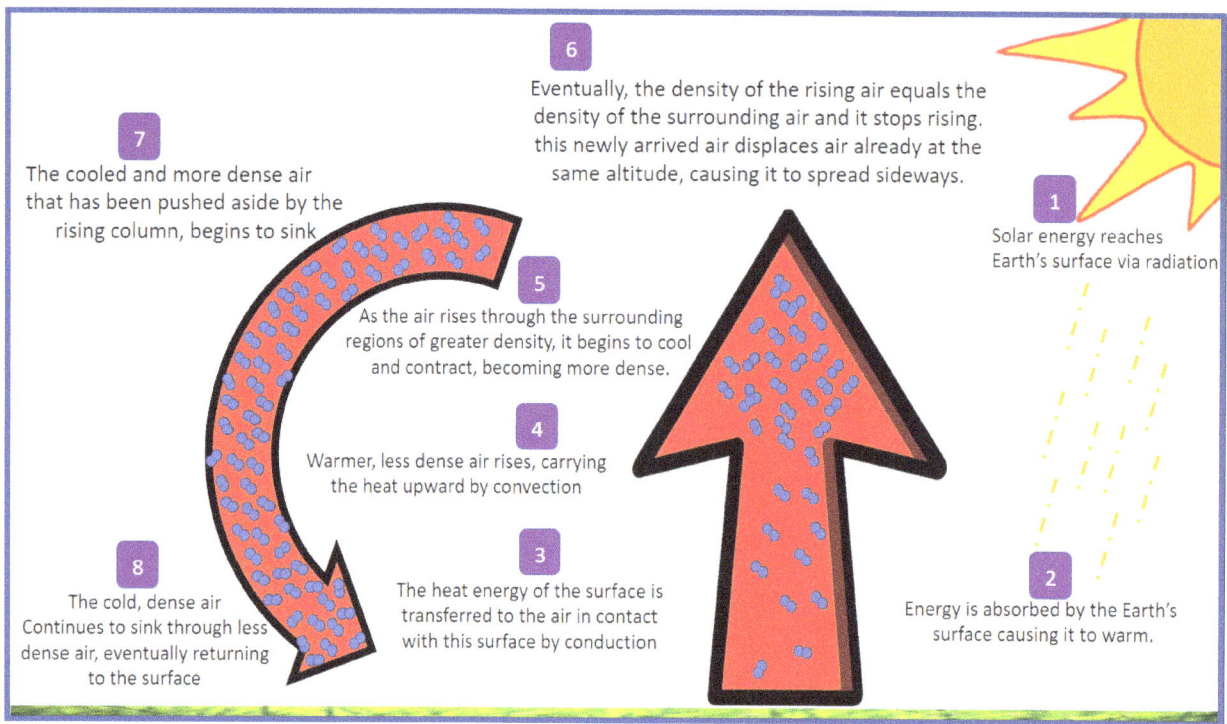

- Radiation: Earth absorbs the heat. Remember it does not heat up uniformly, concrete surface will warm up quicker than grass. Therefore, some areas are hotter than others.
- The energy from that heat is conducted into the air molecules.
- Air molecules that have absorbed that heat move faster and faster and faster. They bounce further apart, conduct heat, and expand.
- When air molecules expand, they are less dense and therefore rise.
- As air rises, something has to replace it. From ALL sides, other air rushes in to fill that gap.
- That is the wind you feel. The wind continues to rise, the 'replacement' air continues to push it up and out.
- Once the rising air hits the stratosphere, it no longer rises (reaching the same density as the air around it) and it fans out in all directions.
- That air cools and now sinks and fans out, and starts the process again by being sucked up after the rising air from the Radiation.

Measuring Wind

The Beaufort Scale shows how the wind speed is estimated by observing the state of the sea.

Points to keep in mind:

1. There may be a lag between the wind getting up and the corresponding sea state.
2. The Beaufort Scale assumes an open ocean, with plenty of fetch.
3. Off a weather shore, the sea state will be less than expected.
4. Don't confuse sea and swell.
5. A weather tide will cause more *lop*. A lee tide will reduce the sea.
6. Heavy rain will smooth the sea surface.

Force (Beaufort scale)	Equivalent speed			Description	Specifications for use at sea
	mph	knots	km/h		
0	0–1	0–1	0–1	Calm	–
1	1–3	1–3	1–5	Light air	Ripples with the appearance of scales are formed, but without foam crests.
2	4–7	4–6	6–11	Light breeze	Small wavelets, still short, but more pronounced. Crests have a glassy appearance.
3	8–12	7–10	12–19	Gentle breeze	Large wavelets. Crests begin to break. Foam of glassy appearance. Perhaps scattered.
4	13–18	11–16	20–28	Moderate breeze	Small waves, becoming larger; fairly frequent white horses.
5	19–24	17–21	29–38	Fresh breeze	Moderate waves, taking a more pronounced, longer form; many white horses are formed. Chance of some spray.
6	25–31	22–27	39–49	Strong breeze	Large waves begin to form; the white foam crests are more extensive everywhere. Probably some spray.
7	32–38	28–33	50–61	Near gale	Sea heaps up and white foam from breaking waves begins to be blown in streaks along the direction of the wind.
8	39–46	34–40	62–74	Gale	Moderately high waves of greater length; edges of crests begin to break into spindrift. The foam is blown in well-marked streaks.
9	47–54	41–47	75–88	Severe gale	High waves. Dense streaks of foam along the direction of the wind. Crests of waves begin to topple, tumble and roll over.
10	55–63	48–55	89–102	Storm	Very high waves with long overhanging crests. The resulting foam, in great patches, is blown in dense white streaks along the direction of the wind. The whole surface of the sea takes on a white appearance. The "tumbling" of the sea becomes more immense and shock-like. Visibility affected.
11	64–72	56–63	103–117	Violent storm	Exceptionally high waves (small and medium-size ships might be, for a time, lost to view behind the waves). The surface is covered with long white patches of foam lying along the direction of the wind. Everywhere, the edges of the wave crests are being blown into froth. Visibility affected.
12	73–83	64–71	118–133	Hurricane	The air is filled with foam and spray. Sea completely white with driving spray; visibility very seriously affected.

The Coriolis Effect

The Coriolis Effect was described by the 19th century French physicist and mathematician Gustave-Gaspard de Coriolis in 1835.

Video: https://www.youtube.com/watch?v=1Y1Qi821n-s

The Coriolis Effect causes a deflection in global wind patterns. Winds flow from highs to lows. As they flow the spinning Earth deflects the winds. In the northern hemisphere, the anticlockwise rotation of Earth deflects the wind to the right and in the southern hemisphere it is deflected to the left.

This is why the wind flows around low pressure systems and high pressure systems in opposing directions in each hemisphere.

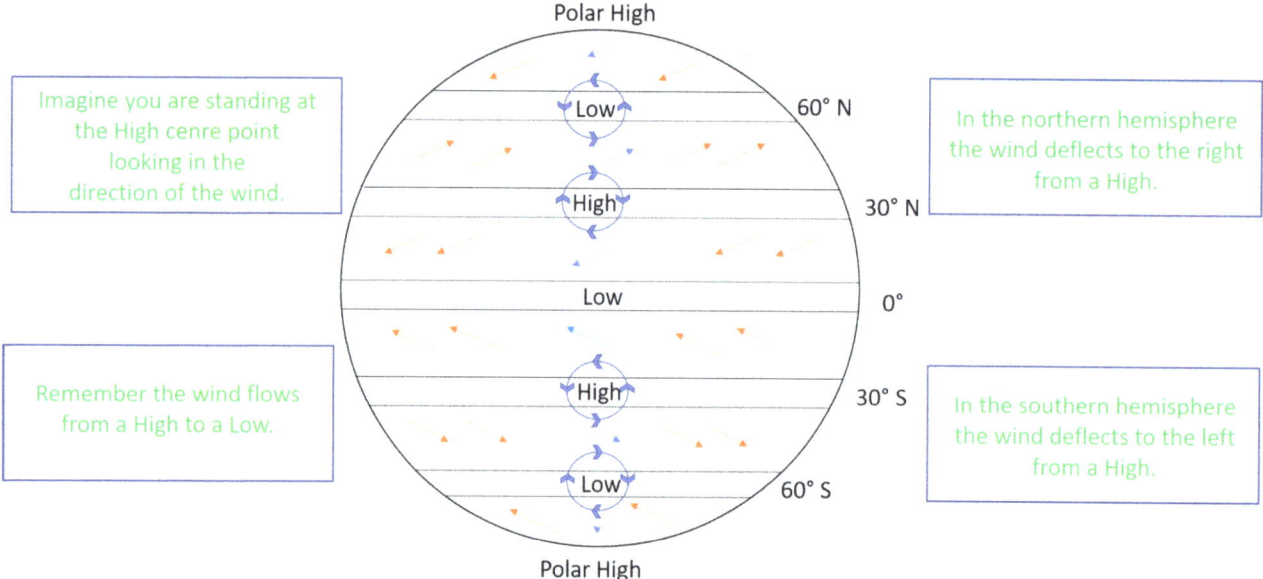

Cycles of Air

The cycles of rising and falling air, coupled with the Earth's rotation, temperatures, humidity and the swirling movement of air masses of various densities provide the different types and variety of climates.

Surface winds are mostly driven by pressure differences, they are measured at about one kilometre above the ground via weather balloons.

Wind blows from areas of high pressure to areas of low pressure. The pressure gradient is an indicator of the speed of the wind.

The deflection of air movement from a high (in the southern hemisphere that is left), results in an anticlockwise rotation, or anticyclone. The air movement is thus clockwise round a low, or cyclone, in the southern hemisphere.

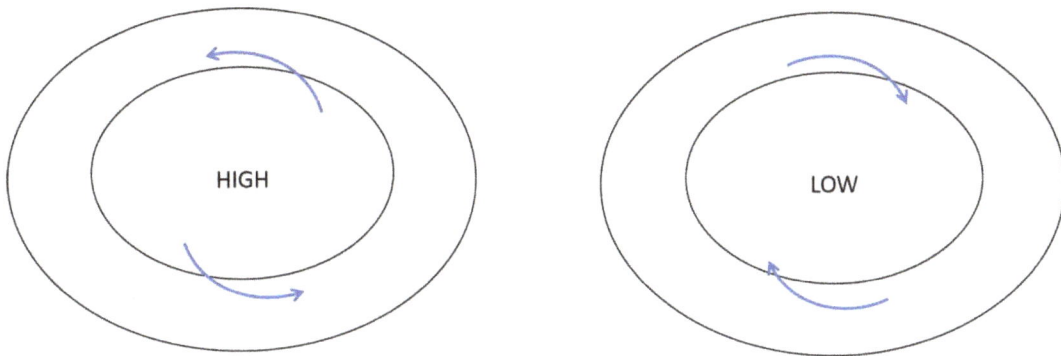

- Wind diverges from the centre of a high and converges towards the centre of a low.
- A *high* is an area of high pressure heavy air which descends and moves outwards from the centre at the surface.
- A *low* is an area of low pressure light air ascending and circulating round it at the surface moves inwards towards the centre.
- Think of the atmosphere as three dimensional. As well as flowing around the pressure systems, air is also rising or sinking within those systems.

Air Pressure and Wind

Air flows from areas of high pressure to areas of low pressure. Therefore, air flows from regions of descending, heavy air to regions of ascending, light air.

- Descending air occurs in clear weather.
- Ascending air happens at fronts and in very warm, wet air (e.g. afternoon thunderstorms).

Wind is caused by air flowing from high pressure to low pressure.
Its direction is influenced by the Earth's rotation

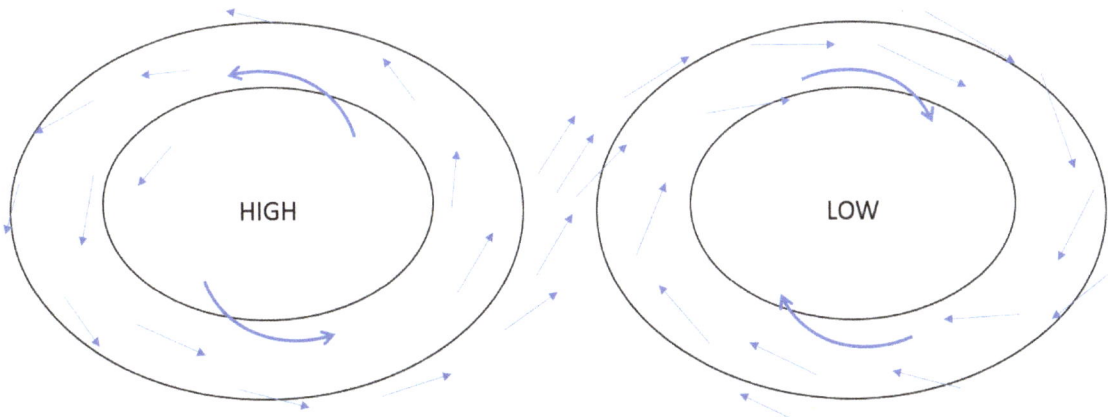

Southern hemisphere wind direction

High pressure systems
- Air is heavy
- Probably falling creating convection
- Air blows outward and anticlockwise across the surface
    (southern hemisphere)

Low pressure systems
- Air is light
- Probably rising creating convection
- Air blows inward and clockwise across the surface
    (southern hemisphere)

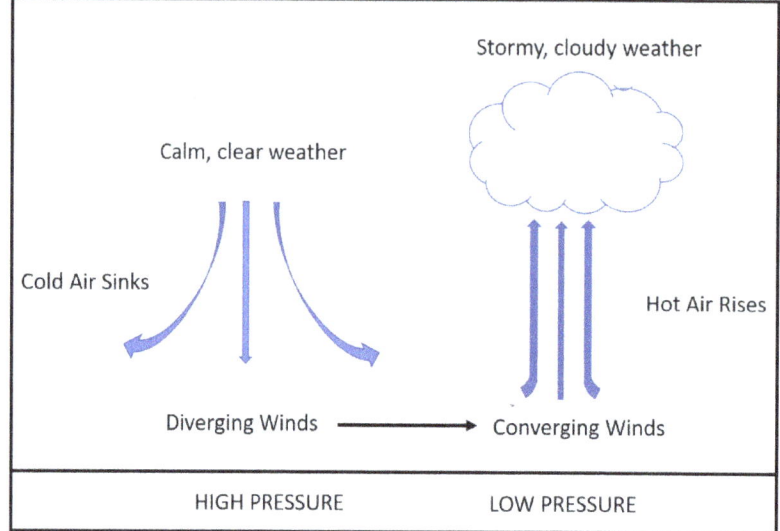

Bringing It Together – Weather Systems and Events

Highs or Anticyclones

Atmospheric pressure is the force exerted by the Earth's atmosphere, in other words the "weight of air".

A High (or anticyclone) is associated with good weather. The centres of highs usually have light winds, good weather with little cloud. The pressure gradient is weak and so the winds are light.

Warm anticyclones are typical of the subtropical oceans and often pass across southern Australia. The central air is warmer than its surroundings. Anticyclones are usually stable and the surface air remains near the surface for long periods. As a result, the amount of water vapour and pollutants increase creating stratiform cloud, fog and smog in the outer regions of the high.

Cold anticyclones form over winter continents, (e.g. Siberia and Canada). They are caused by intense surface cooling, resulting in increased air density and therefore higher pressure. The central weather is typically crisp, clear and very cold. (In contrast, very clear weather is associated with low pressure systems, where the air is generally ascending, and taking all the pollution away from the surface.)

Ridges and Troughs

The diagrams below show isobars and pressure gradients in simple format. An isobar is a line on a weather map that joins a place of having the same atmospheric pressure. The pressure gradient (the space between the isobars) informs us of the strength of wind and the direction. The closer the isobars are the steeper the gradient. This means stronger winds in the direction parallel (or near parallel) to the isobars.

Ridge

A ridge is an area of high pressure extending into or penetrating an area of low pressure. A ridge of high pressure may extend out from an anticyclone. Ridges tend to bring in warmer and drier weather as they approach.

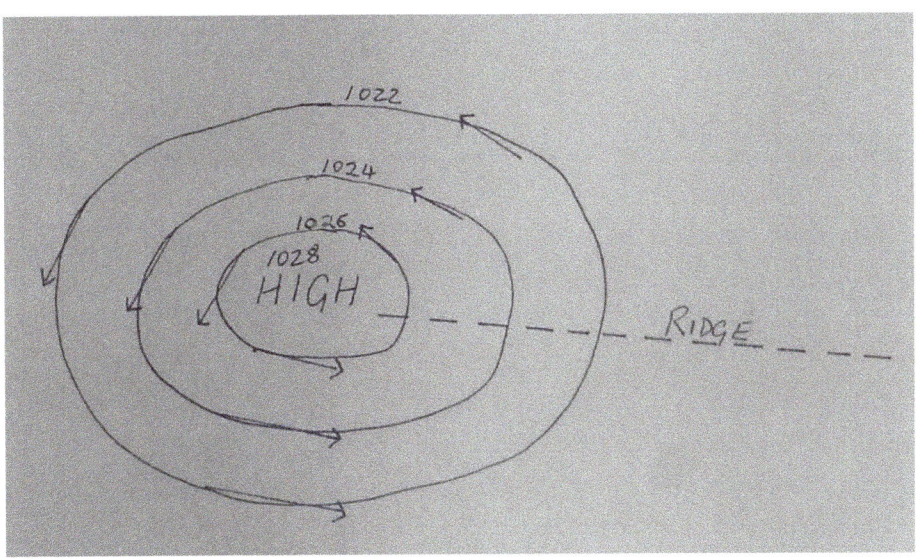

Ridge - What does this mean to the sailor?

Ridges are an elongation of the high. Because of the sharper curvature of isobars associated with the ridge, the wind direction will shift quickly across the ridge axis more quickly than in other portions of the circulation of winds in the high. The sailor must be very alert to this variability and be prepared to respond quickly.

Depression or Low

A low pressure system is an area of low atmospheric pressure within a closed system of isobars. The air is light and is therefore rising from its centre into the upper atmosphere which allows more surface air to flow in towards its centre. Lows 'carry off' moisture and pollution from the Earth's surface, creating clouds and strong winds. Gradient wind blows parallel to isobars clockwise (assuming no friction). A cyclone is an area of intense low pressure (the low deepens) which usually form over tropical waters, usually in the summer months.

Trough

A trough is an area of low pressure extending into an area of high pressure. A trough of low pressure may extend out from a depression.

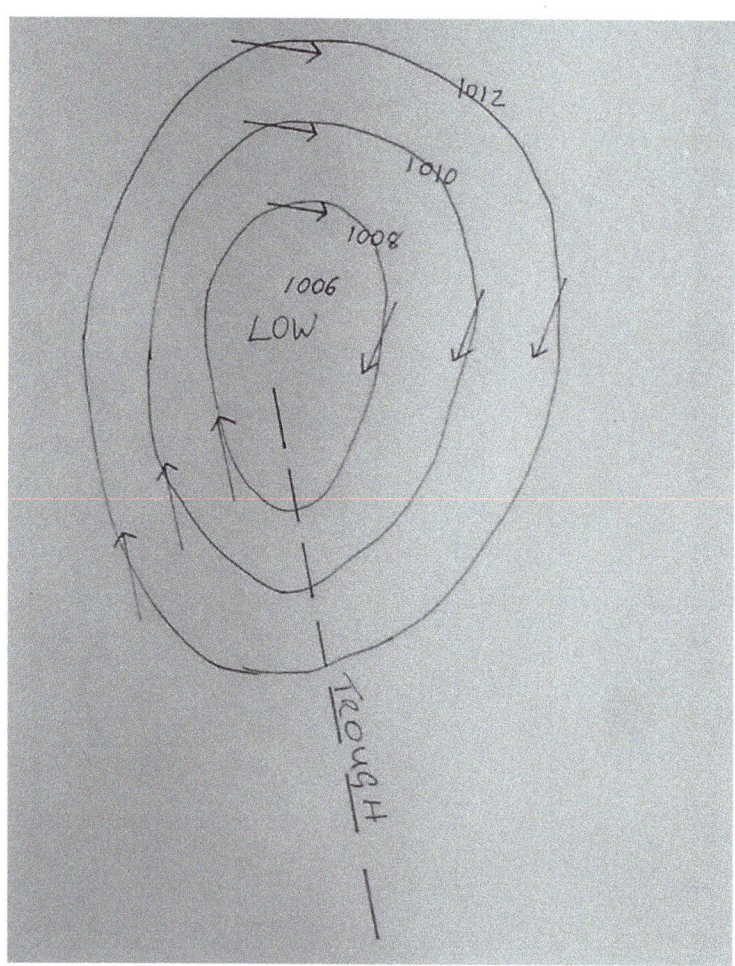

Most troughs bring clouds, showers, and a wind shift, and cold air mass. Troughs tend to bring in cooler and cloudier weather as they approach.

Trough - What Does This Mean to Us?
Another elongation in isobars. Which means squally weather and could mean a sharp wind change and squalls.

Ridges/Troughs in Our Experience
With troughs and ridges we experienced enhanced winds and variable winds (above and below the forecast). They are phenomena to be aware of, which is why you should check synoptic charts. They can cause a sharp 'blip' in isobars. Whenever we were close to one of those 'blips' we always suffered short, sharp, severe weather.

Air Masses and Global Air Circulation
The circulation of air across the globe prevents the equatorial region from becoming too hot and the polar regions becoming too cold. Air temperature dictates whether a region is humid or dry or hot or cold.

Air masses are a body of air. They can be over water or land. A body of air will have uniform characteristics. They are linked to global wind patterns and defined as large areas of air that are similar in temperature and humidity.

Australia's air circulation is dominated by high pressure systems which provides our warm, dry climate. These high pressure systems move with the seasons leading to the Australian seasonal rainfall patterns. For example, Tropical Maritime Air: Air over a tropical ocean is warmed from below and absorbs moisture from the sea surface. Typically, this produces trade wind weather and increasing stratus-type clouds as the air is cooled from below as it moves into higher latitudes.

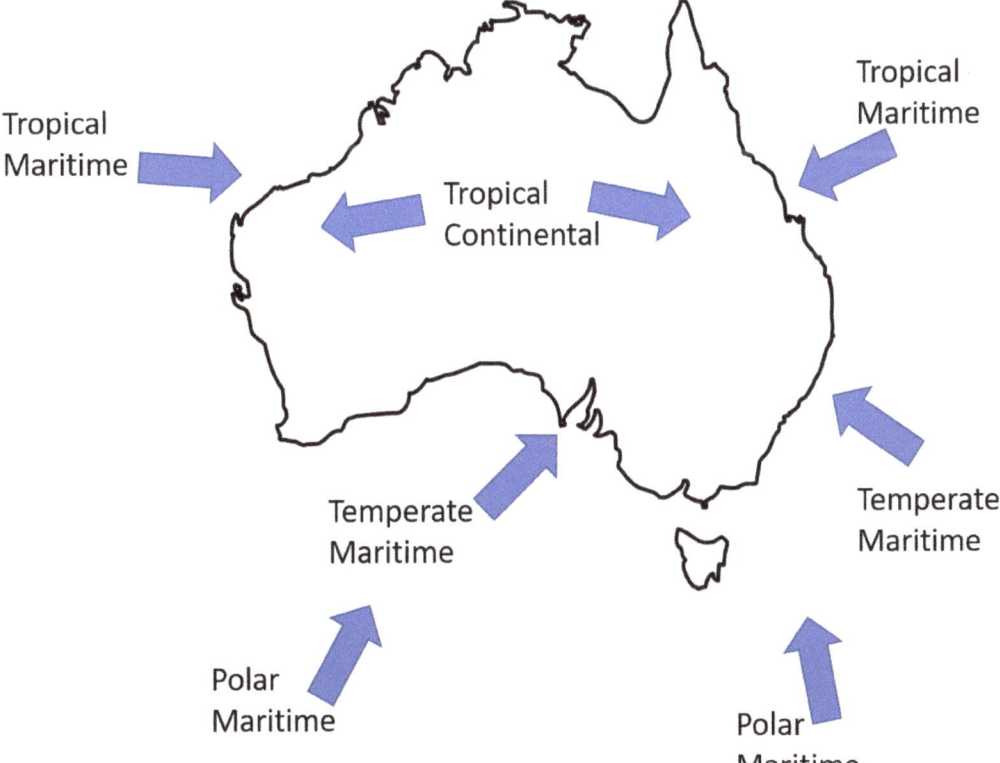

Air masses are classified by their source, whether equatorial, tropical, polar or Antarctic, and further designated maritime or continental.

The properties of the most common air masses are:

- Tropical Maritime Warm moist
- Tropical Continental Hot and dry
- Temperate Maritime Cool and moist
- Polar Maritime Cold and moist

Air and the weather associated with it is often uniform when passing over a region, marked weather changes will take place at the front, or frontal zone between two adjacent air masses.

Frontal Depressions

When two air masses of different temperature and moisture meet (e.g. polar and tropical air masses) they form a boundary called a *front*. Friction between the two air masses along the front produces differing speeds for the differing air masses. This creates waves along the front as one air mass invades the other.

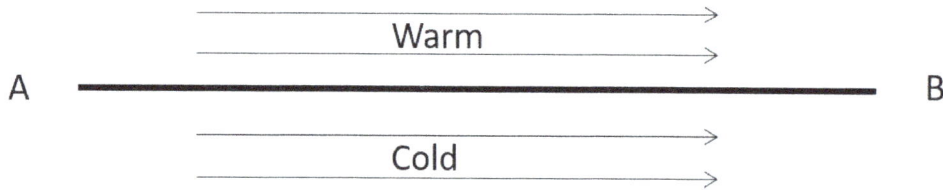

The warm and cold air masses meet, the boundary line is A-B

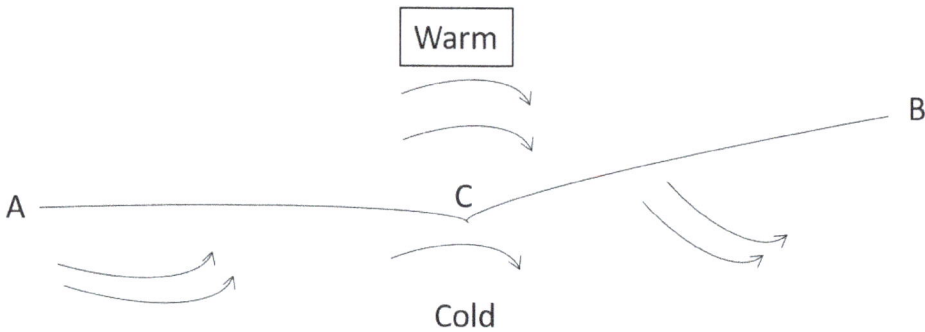

At some locations, the warmer air mass moves faster than the colder one and usually becomes the aggressor, pushing into and overriding the cold air mass.

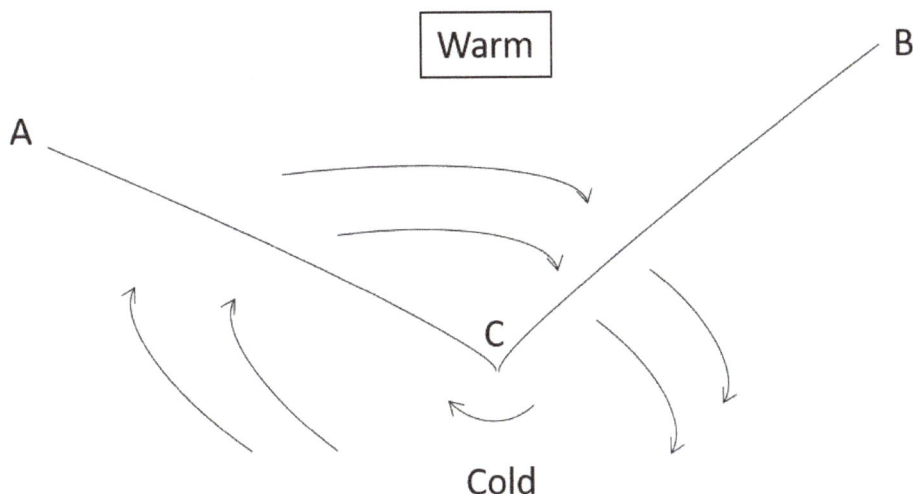

However, the cold air mass, in Australia, is usually more aggressive and pushes into the warmer air, under-cutting it.

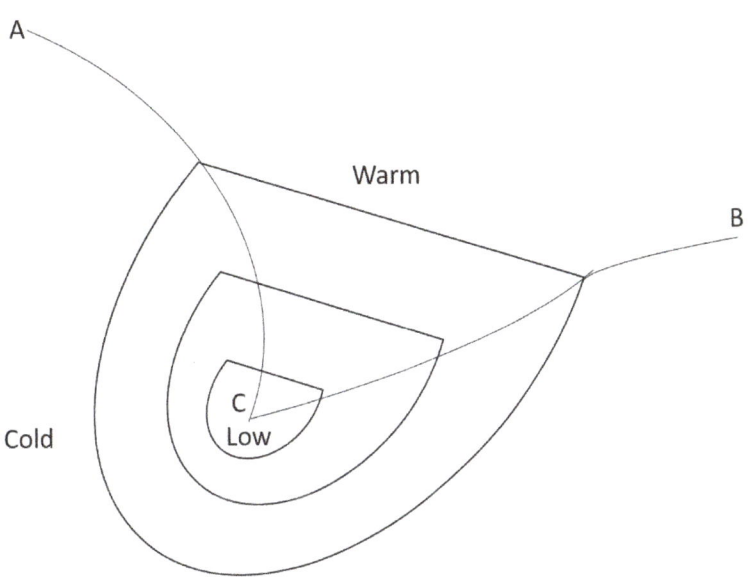

The barometric pressure drops as the air masses interact. A rotating wind develops where the cold air pushes and under-cuts the warm air, and where the warmer air overrides the cold air.

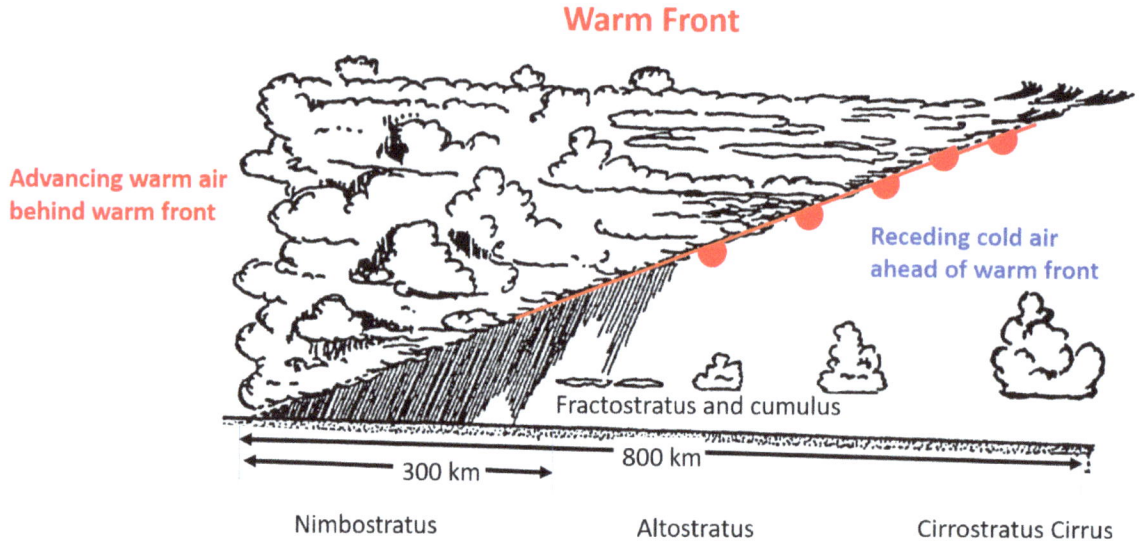

This is a frontal depression. In Australia, the warm front is often weak and almost non-existent. Our weather maps often only show a well-defined cold front.

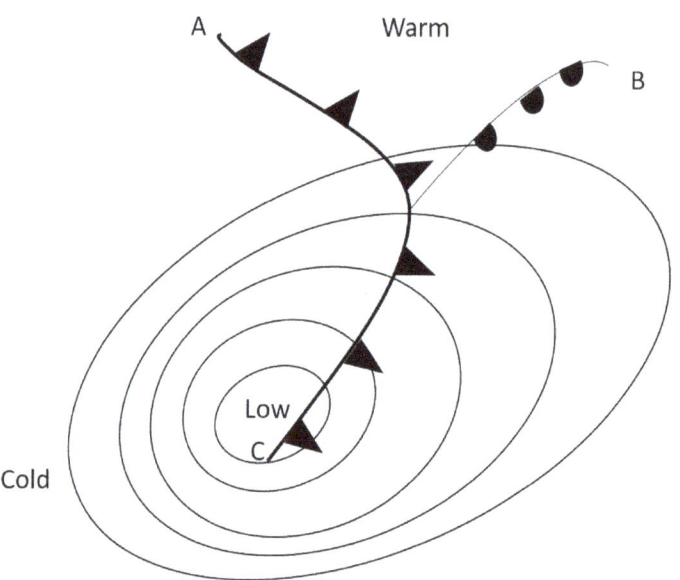

Cold Fronts and Warm Fronts What does this mean to us?
In Australia, the cold front is most important to us as mariners. They are more common and the weather associated with a cold front can be severe.

Cold Fronts

Early Signs: A significant drop in the barometer and large Cumulous clouds aligned along the leading edge of the front. The result of the warm moist air rising so steeply it may create towering Cumulous clouds with the distinctive anvil on top.

Occasionally in the summer months, though, a southerly change (cold front) can occur without any cloud and a violent southerly buster can be created from more serious cold fronts.

Most of the Southerly Busters occur between September and March in southeast Australia, most frequently in Victoria and New South Wales, although they are less frequent in the north of New South Wales – they typically arrive late afternoon or evening. They also occur on the east coast of Tasmania, New Zealand, Argentina, and Chile.

Cold fronts are usually short and sharp because of their steep slope (The warm air that is pushed up by the advancing cold air creates a vertical lift and therefore a much steeper slope than a warm front) On average, cold fronts stretch out over around 30 miles but the wind speed can reach in excess of 40 knots. Thunderstorm and heavy showers can accompany the fronts. The air behind a cold front is colder as it is blowing from the south.

> A note for boaters
> In our experience, fronts are generally longer than indicated on synoptic charts. We have often thought we'd miss the front, only to be affected by it.

Occluded Fronts

The occluded front occurs when a cold front overtakes a warm front. As with the warm front, occluded fronts are quite rare over the Australian continent but can sometimes be seen over the Southern Ocean on satellite photographs.

Jet Streams

Jet streams are like rivers of wind in the upper levels of the atmosphere. These fairly narrow strips of strong winds have a huge influence on climate, as they can push air masses around and affect weather patterns. They are formed by temperature differences in the upper atmosphere, between the cold polar air and the warm tropical air. This abrupt change in temperature causes a large pressure difference, which forces the air to move quickly.

Jet streams follow the boundaries between warm and cool air. The winds blow from west to east in jet streams (due to the Earth's rotation) but the flow often shifts to the north and south. (The motion of the air is not directly north and south, but it is affected by the momentum and how fast a location on or above the Earth moves relative to the Earth's axis, that is if you stand on the equator, you are moving faster than someone standing near to a pole. The jet streams also collide which alters their path).

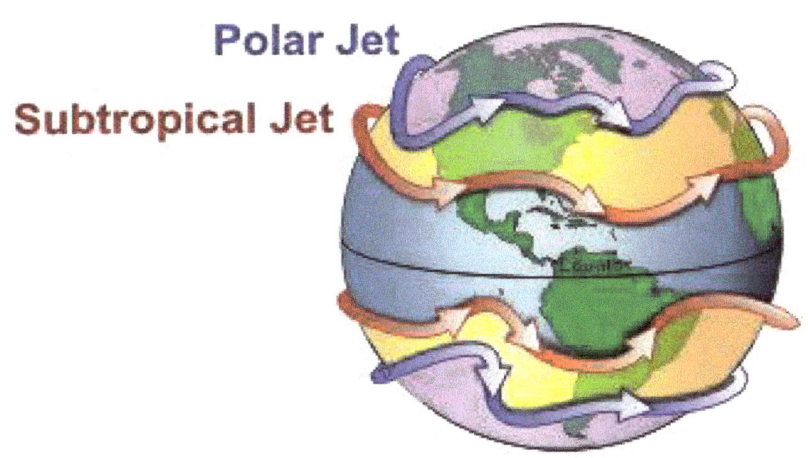

Jet Streams – What They Mean to Us

To understand how a jet stream can affect us, as boaters, here's a quote from G. Bruce Knecht, author of *The Proving Ground* about the catastrophic Sydney to Hobart race in 1998.

"The main wild card was the course of polar jet streams. Predicting the exact course of jet streams, high-speed rivers of air that travel 9,000 metres above the Earth's surface and change direction as they collide with one another, is difficult. But while polar jet streams generally don't extend far enough north to reach Bass Strait during the summer, satellite photographs of high-level cloud formations and weather balloon observations suggested that one stream might do so during the race. A jet stream straddling the low would intensify it by setting off a dangerous chain reaction: the high-altitude wind would siphon the warm air out from the centre of the low, further reducing the pressure at the core of the storm and speeding the rush of wind toward the low – and accelerating the system's clockwise movement."

This is a book well worth reading for both the skilful writing and the additional learning/information.

Jet steams can upset the 'usual' weather patterns. For example, in the 2017 Atlantic Rally for Cruisers (ARC) the participants beat into head winds for some time, which was an unexpected and unusual weather pattern. The cause was a large depression west of the Canary Islands, blocking the route west and preventing the trade winds from reaching south. This feature was linked to the jet stream.

In 2017 in Australia, while stormy weather hit Perth, summer arrived early to the east coast. This extreme weather was linked to jet streams. In Australia, the jet stream is a westerly wind that sometimes dips. The dip in 2017 caused cooler south-south-westerly winds to travel further north than usual. This brought along cold fronts for Perth and when a corresponding dip occurs in the east, hot northerly desert air arrives into Brisbane and Sydney.

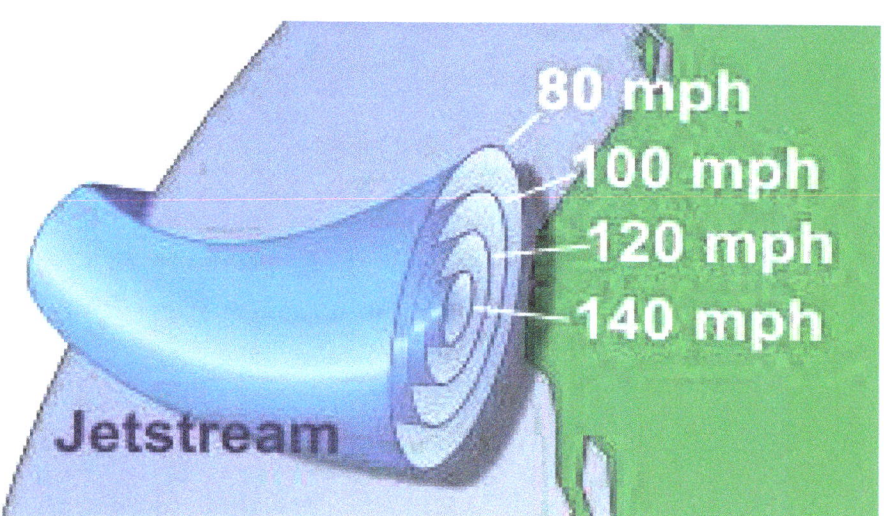

Jet streams are often indicated by a line on a weather map indicating the location of the strongest wind. But remember that jet streams are wider and not as distinct as a single line, they are actually regions where the wind speed increases towards a central core of greatest strength.

Forecasting Frontal Weather

Weather fronts cause clouds to form. Fronts occur when two large masses of air collide.

Warm fronts produce many different cloud types (when the warm air slides over the cold air and replaces it): altocumulus, altostratus, cirrocumulus, cirrostratus, cirrus, cumulonimbus (and associated mammatus clouds), nimbostratus, stratus, and stratocumulus.

Cold fronts occur when the warm air is displaced and pushed up by the heavy cold air. Cumulus clouds are the most common cloud types, that often grow into cumulonimbus clouds, producing thunderstorms. Other clouds such as nimbostratus, stratocumulus, and stratus clouds can be produced by cold fronts.

Here's a general observation chart:

48 hours prior.	Small Cumulus or clear sky.	Fine, northeast wind.
24 hours prior.	Possibly medium Cumulus, Cirrus invading the sky from the west.	Fine, northerly gusty winds.
12 hours prior.	Overcast Cirrus or Cirrostratus, large Cumulus.	Possibly some showers, strong north-westerly winds.
6 hour prior.	Overcast Cirrus or Cirrostratus, some alto Cumulus, large Cumulus and some Cumulonimbus.	Some showers, possibly lightning to west and southwest, strong north-westerly winds.
Time of front.	Cirrus, Altocumulus, Altostratus, large Cumulus and Cumulonimbus.	Showers, squalls and storms, wind backing to the southwest.
After front.	Cumulus, Stratocumulus and Altostratus clearing.	Showers and rain clearing, cooler southerly or southeasterly winds.

East Coast Lows

These are a phenomenon that occur over southern Queensland and eastern New South Wales, usually between latitudes 25°S to 40°S. They usually occur in the autumn or winter with an average frequency of ten significant impact Maritime lows per year. They are small and often develop very rapidly.

East coast lows are classified into three types according to where they form within the easterly dip (an easterly dip provides an influx of moist air from the Coral Sea via a low pressure trough extending southwards from QLD into inland NSW.) The first type form to the west of the trough line. The second type form on the trough line and the third type form to the east of the trough line. Such lows often develop very rapidly and have been responsible for extremely strong winds and floods along the east coast from southern Queensland to the Victorian border.

While there are three distinct types, all have characteristics in common:

- The formation of severe east coast cyclones usually occurs at night near the coast in a region of strong oceanic temperature gradients.
- Night-time formation is more usual because continental cooling enhances the temperature gradients along the coast and a strong temperature gradient near the surface seems necessary to maintain the strength of a low.
- If east coast lows move away from the coast, they rapidly weaken.
- A distinct eye occurs just as in a tropical cyclone and wind speeds often reach hurricane force.

Video: https://www.abc.net.au/news/2018-12-26/sydney-to-hobart-1998-east-coast-low-changed-marine-forecasting/10286796

Katabatic Winds

Katabatic wind is from the Greek word *Katabaino*, which means *to go down*. They are down-flowing winds from high elevations such as mountains.

They are caused by forces that are the result of temperature differences induced by the local topography. They are most strongly developed when the synoptic pressure gradient is small such as during anticyclonic weather.

If you are anchored near mountainous or hilly areas, during the day, differential warming of the landscape occurs. During the afternoon depending on the steepness of the valleys. Katabatic winds can be strong and at times destructive.

Local Weather Patterns

As the land changes temperature throughout the day a pattern of land and sea breezes is created along the coast. The pattern occurs as follows:

Sea Breeze

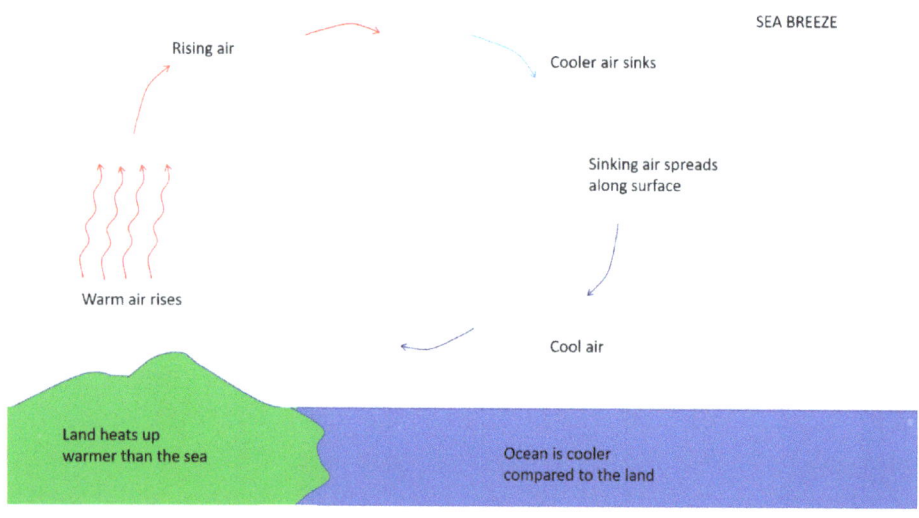

During the day, the sun heats the land. The air is in contact with the land and so is heated too (conduction) and as this air is heated it rises (convection). The air above the water remains cooler and therefore flows onto the land replacing the warm (heated) air that has risen. This is commonly called a sea breeze: the wind that flows from the sea. Maximum strength of the sea breeze occurs about mid-afternoon. As the heat goes out of the day the sea breeze will lessen towards the evening. With minimal pressure gradient, the sea breeze will generally average 15-18 knots and will not extend more than 20 miles from the coast.

Land Breeze

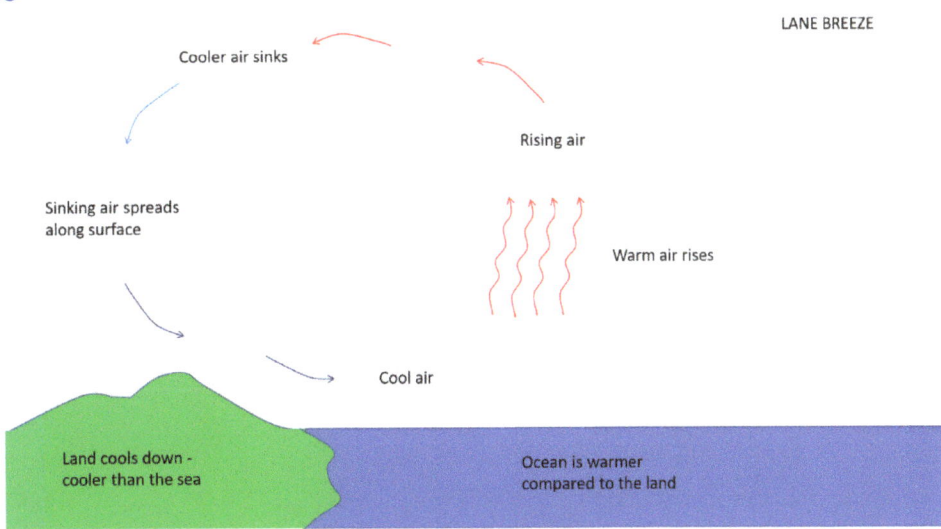

At night, the opposite effect occurs. The land cools down and so the cool air flows downhill from the land and out to sea. This displaces the comparatively warmer air over the water. This land breeze (from the land) is usually gentle (about 4-6 knots) and does not usually extend more than 5-10 nautical miles out to sea.

The Effect of Land and Sea-Breezes on Gradient Wind – What It Means to Us

If the gradient or trade wind is onshore the sea breeze effect can be quite strong.

For coastal sailing mariners, the most important effect is the land breeze during the early morning, which can interrupt the prevailing trade winds.

As the air closest to the ground cools it settles in layers like a thick blanket that may only be a couple of hundred metres thick. Along the coast and over the land the warmer gradient wind flows over the top of this layer. This layer is known as an *inversion layer* and will exist until the sun begins to heat the land and restores the normal vertical temperature profile in the atmosphere.

Coastal waters forecasts will often mention trade winds being lighter inshore at night and in the early morning. Also, as evidence of this effect, late at night in the moonlight look for low-level clouds moving much faster than the air speed at ground level would suggest.

Equatorial Trough/Intertropical Convergence Zone (ITCZ)

The Equatorial Trough and ITCZ are often use synonymously. The Equatorial Trough is a line of low pressure between the trade winds of the two hemispheres.

The Intertropical Convergence Zone (ITCZ), is the boundary where the northeast and southeast trade winds converge.

Although its specific position varies seasonally (and for other reasons such as land mass vs sea area), it encircles Earth near the equator, and it is a trough of low pressure.

The pressure gradient between this trough and the subtropical highs in both hemispheres creates a force pushing air from the highs towards the equator. Deflection of this air occurs with the Coriolis Effect, resulting in north-easterly wind north of the equator and southeasterly wind south of the equator.

Put simply, it can be defined as a single simple low pressure system trough stretching around the globe, it is extremely complex with a structure which varies over time.

The ITCZ is also known by sailors as the doldrums or the calms because of its lack of wind.

(Note: you may read ITCZ – Intertropical Convergence Zone and ITZC – Intertropical Zone of Convergence – it's just a preference, both are the same.)

A wide range of weather conditions can be associated with the ITCZ. If the trades the weak and there is no convergence there may be virtually no cloud or weather activity associated with it. But if the trades intensify, large masses of Cumulonimbus may develop resulting with heavy rainfall.

El Niño La Niña

The terms El Niño and La Niña refer to periodic changes in Pacific Ocean sea surface temperatures that have impacts on weather all over the globe.

Australia's weather is influenced by many climate drivers. El Niño and La Niña have perhaps the strongest influence on year-to-year climate variability in Australia. They are a part of a natural cycle known as the El Niño–Southern Oscillation (ENSO) and are associated with a sustained period (many months) of warming (El Niño) or cooling (La Niña) in the central and eastern tropical Pacific. The ENSO cycle loosely operates over timescales from one to eight years.

Potential effects of El Niño on Australia include:
- Reduced rainfall
- Warmer temperatures
- *Shift in temperature extremes
- Increased frost risk
- Reduced tropical cyclone numbers
- Later monsoon onset
- Increased fire danger in southeast Australia
- Decreased alpine snow depths

La Niña typically means:
- Increased rainfall
- Cooler maximum temperatures
- **Shift in temperature extremes
- Decreased frost risk
- Greater tropical cyclone numbers
- Earlier monsoon onset
- Deeper relative snow cover

* For temperature extremes, there are three different measures of heat that are relevant to El Niño: wide-area heatwaves; single-day extremes at specific point locations; and long-duration warm spells. The relationship of El Niño with each of these elements may be location dependent and quite different. During the warmer half of the year, during an El Niño year, there are fewer stationary high pressure systems. This means that for coastal locations in the south, e.g. Adelaide and Melbourne, individual daily heat extremes tend to be hotter during an El Niño year with a reduced frequency of prolonged warm spells. El Niño is associated with both an increase in individual extreme hot days and multi-day warm spells further north. Although maximum temperatures are generally warmer than average during El Niño years, decreased cloud cover often leads to cooler than average temperatures during the night, particularly across eastern Australia.

** The cooler than average daytime temperatures during La Niña years is often associated with a decreased frequency of extreme daily high temperatures. In the warmer half of the year, southern coastal locations such as Adelaide and Melbourne experience fewer individual daily heat extremes during La Niña years but an increased frequency of prolonged warm spells.

The Indian Ocean Dipole (IOD)

The dipole is a climate phenomenon similar to El Niño and is sometimes called "Indian Niño" due to the similarity to its Pacific equivalent. The Indian Ocean dipole refers to the difference in sea surface temperatures in opposite parts of the Indian Ocean.

A positive Indian Ocean Dipole means a wetter west and drier east.
- There is more rainfall over East African countries (the rainfall often moves with the warm waters).
- In the eastern part of the Indian Ocean, there will be reduced rainfall and sea surface temperatures are cooler than normal.

A negative dipole phase is the opposite
- More rain and warmer water in the east of the Indian Ocean, while the west will experience cooler and drier conditions.

When sea temperatures are close to average, the dipole is in neutral phase.

In 2019, a strong positive dipole resulted in more rainfall and floods in eastern Africa and droughts in southeast Asia and Australia.

Thunderstorms

Thunderstorms consist of abrupt fluctuations of pressure, temperature, and wind. produced by Cumulonimbus clouds. These clouds can move in a different direction to the prevailing wind.

Thunderstorms can create a hazard especially for smaller vessels due to the front of storm blowing out strong, gusty winds.

Lightning is a discharge of electricity between the cloud and sea (or land). Thunder and lightning occur together but we see the flash before we hear the thunder.

Developing Thunderstorms

Look for cumulus clouds (like cotton wool) that are growing larger. This cloud will have four features:
- The top of the cloud will be shaped like an anvil.
- The main body is tall with 'cauliflower' sides.
- Roll clouds will develop along the leading edge of the base.
- A dark area extends from the cloud's base towards the ground.

Sometimes the storm moves in the direction that the anvil appears to be pointing.

Tornados and Waterspouts

The difference between a tornado and waterspout is that a tornado forms over land, while the waterspout forms over water. They are both classified as tornados, with a waterspout being a type of tornado.

Tornados are off-shoots of tall cumulus clouds, and have a rapid rotation of air. A waterspout tends to be weaker than the land-based tornado.

The water inside a waterspout is formed by condensation in the cloud. There are two major types of waterspouts: tornadic waterspouts and fair-weather waterspouts. Tornadic waterspouts start as true tornados. Influenced by winds associated with severe thunderstorms, air rises and rotates on a vertical axis. Fair weather waterspouts form in light wind conditions so they normally move very little.

Waterspouts, heavy with water, usually fall apart after thirty minutes.

Wind - Apparent & True

When your boat is moving, the wind indicator (or your wetted thumb) shows apparent wind. This means that the direction and strength of the wind includes your movement, that is if you are going downwind, the wind feels weaker, but if you are going into the wind, it feels stronger. True wind is the actual force of the wind if you were stationary. Try to give your true wind when talking to other boats.

Wind Vectors

Step by step: how to calculate true wind:

1. Draw a line representing your true course and speed, for example, course 000° T, speed 5 knots. Choose a scale to use, say 5 centimetres for 5 knots (one cm per knot).

2. Place an arrow at the head of the line where your bow is pointing.

3. Draw the apparent wind speed and direction, that is where the wind is blowing to, with the head of the arrow pointing at the stern of your course and speed line. In our example, that is approximately 040° off the ship's bow at 10 knots, therefore the line would be ten centimetres long. (The drawing below is not to scale.)

4. The true wind is the resultant vector drawn from the tail of the apparent wind line to the head of your vessel's course and speed line.

5. Measure the true wind line using the scale you have been using for the rest of the vector (in this example, measure how many centimetres the true wind line is, that will be your true wind speed in knots).

6. Measure the angle of the true wind. You now have the true wind speed and direction.

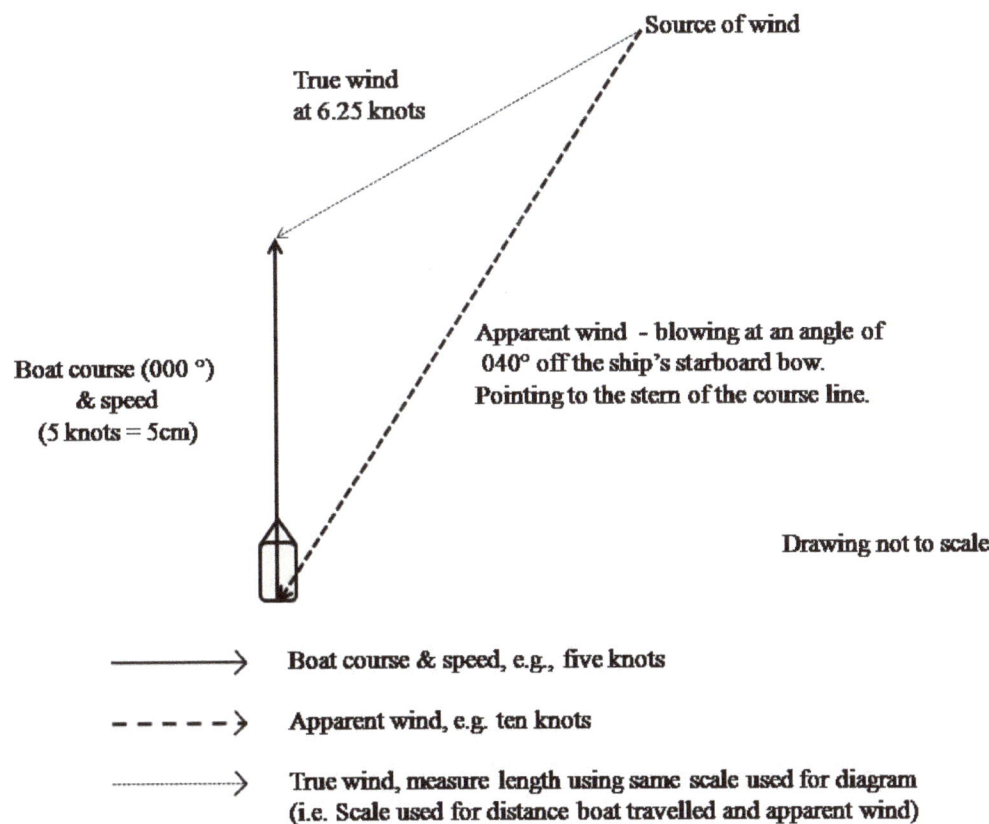

Rules to follow:

1. Speed is always drawn to the same scale for each line of the vector.

2. Direction is always drawn in the same type of bearing, for example, true, magnetic or compass.

3. True is best, then you can calculate the true wind (direction the vessel is going to and direction the wind is coming from).

4. The head of the arrow must be placed at the head of the line, indicating direction.

5. Apparent wind blows to your stern (on your course and speed line).

6. True wind blows to your bow (on your course and speed arrow).

Tropical Revolving Storms (TRS) or Tropical Cyclones

Tropical cyclones are violent. They generate extreme winds and flooding rains. Conditions are extremely dangerous for vessels at sea and in harbours.

The eye or centre of a cyclone produces a temporary lull in the wind, but then is replaced by extreme winds in the opposite direction (to their direction experience prior to the eye).

In the northern part of Australia, cyclone season is from November to April.

Development of a Cyclone

Cyclones start off as an intense low that originates in the tropics, that deepens into cyclones as it travels away from the equator.

Cyclones do not form within five degrees of the equator as there is not enough Coriolis Effect. The wind cannot deflect and therefore form a circular motion.

- Sea surface temperature must be a minimum of 27° C
- A low pressure area over the ocean
- Surface winds converge around an eye (requires a jet stream in the upper atmosphere)
- The Coriolis Effect

Video: https://www.youtube.com/watch?v=UKL9NIxLIIE

Warning Signs

The most significant indicator that a cyclone is possible is a definite, unusually steep fall in the barometric pressure. If the corrected pressure is more than 3 hPa below normal, beware! If it is more than 5 hPa below normal, there is probably a storm within 200 miles. When checking the barometer to see if it is below normal, it is essential to take into account the diurnal variation.

The falling barometer is the most significant indicator. The remaining warning signs are useful, but not conclusive on their own.

Long heavy swell from the direction of the storm is a good long range indicator (hundreds of miles) and may not be in keeping with the weather at the time, for example, a heavy NE swell while the wind is SE at 10-15 kn.

A lurid (odd coloured) sky. This is caused by ice crystals in the upper atmosphere radiating out from the centre of the storm giving the effect of a high-level horizontal rainbow.

A heavy, humid, and oppressive atmosphere.

Unusual behaviour by sea birds. They will either stay ashore and roost all day or disappear altogether.

An appreciable change in the direction and strength of the wind.

Three Stages of a Cyclone
1. Tropical Depression: usually less than 33 knots of wind, swirling clouds and rain
2. Tropical Storm: 34 -63 knots of wind
3. Tropical Cyclone: greater than 64 knots of wind

When winds reach gale force (or above) they are formally designated a cyclone and given a name.

Tracking a Cyclone
https://www.youtube.com/watch?v=QjZfXrv7FEE
Tropical cyclones develop over tropical waters around Australia during the warmer months, mostly November to April. The BOM provides warning services for these cyclones. Warnings are issued for land-based communities under threat and for mariners. Routine outlooks are also issued during the cyclone season.

AUSTRALIAN AREAS
Australia's area of responsibility for cyclone services is divided between three Tropical Cyclone Warning Centres (TCWCs): Perth, Darwin and Brisbane.

Cyclone Paths
The path of a cyclone is parabolic. In the southern hemisphere, they usually move towards west/southwest aided by the Coriolis Effect, they then curve towards the southeast. The system's speed has an average of 10 knots (or less) before it recurves and then increased to 15 knots after recurving. But cyclones have variable and erratic behaviours and can be completely unpredictable.

Winds are usually stronger on the southeast side as they are moving in the same direction as the eye. Winds on the north-western side are going in the opposite way of the movement of the cyclone. It is possible to identify a non-navigable (more dangerous) semicircle and a navigable semicircle. (Study the following diagram).

Non-navigable and Navigable Semicircle

If you are cruising in a cyclone area during cyclone season, ensure you understand the usual behaviour of the storm within your location. Analyse the best track to sail should you be caught in a cyclone. Note that in the northeast of Australia, cyclones generally move in a southwesterly direction before curving towards the south or southeast (but there are no guarantees).

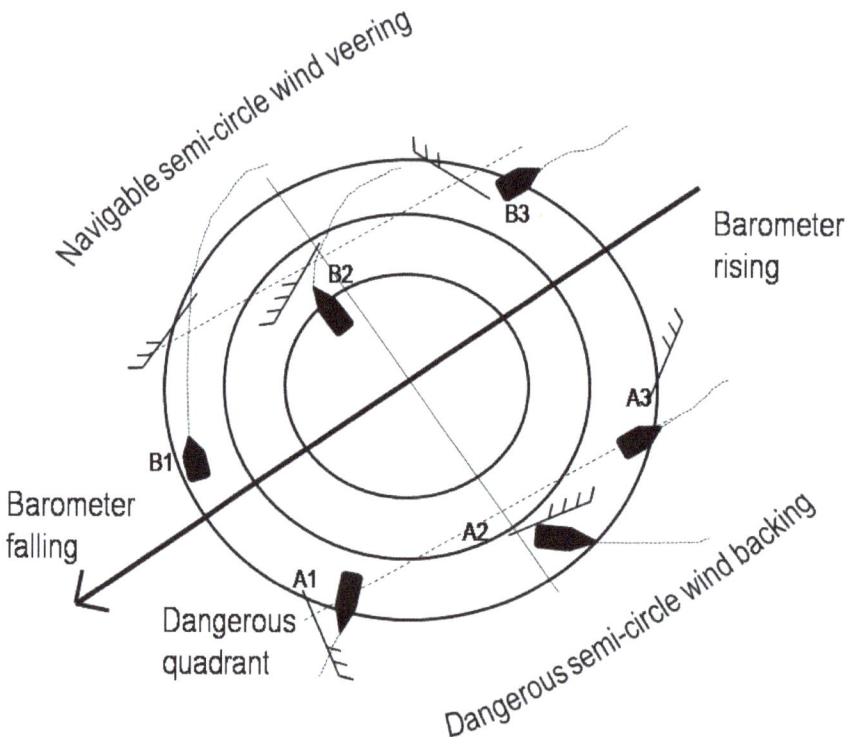

This picture is based on cyclones in the southern hemisphere. (Cyclones spin clockwise in the southern hemisphere, anticlockwise in the northern hemisphere.) Therefore, the dangerous semicircle of a cyclone is to the right of an approaching cyclone path. This area has the strongest winds and it is the direction the cyclone is expected to move.

Vessels at B1, B2 and B3 have a chance to run away from the vortex. Vessels at A1, A2 and A3 are in a perilous situation: if they run they will be sucked into the vortex. Therefore, they have to keep the wind on the port bow to try to get away from the vortex. Conditions will improve, believe it or not, by A3. From here keep heading northeast until the cyclone dies out.

To Evade a Cyclone

In the southern hemisphere, if you are in the navigable semicircle, keep the wind on your port quarter and manoeuvre away from the cyclone. If you are in the dangerous semicircle, keep the wind on your port bow and try to manoeuvre away from the vortex.

Remember, no part of a cyclone is safe. It is just that in the navigable sectors you have a better chance of escaping the path of the vortex.

If you are unable to seek shelter, you must give the cyclone as wide a berth as possible. To do this maintain a continuous plot of the cyclone's track by plotting the positions of its centre. From each successive position of its centre draw an angle of 40° on each side of its forecast path. This will allow for the possibility of the cyclone deviating from its path. Then draw a curve between these lines (that you've just drawn) equal to forty-eight-hours of its speed. For example, if the storm is travelling at 10 knots, draw the curve at 48 x 10 = 480 nautical miles. Plan your route outside this area, updating as soon as (and every time) you have new information.

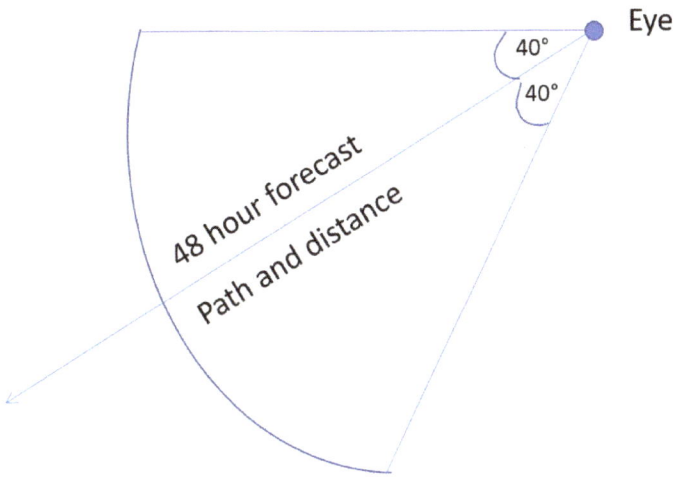

Angle of Indraft

The wind cuts across the isobars at an 'Angle of Indraft'. It results from a balance of Pressure Gradient Force, Coriolis Effect, and friction.

The angle of draft varies from around 45° at the edge of a cyclone to 0° in the eye

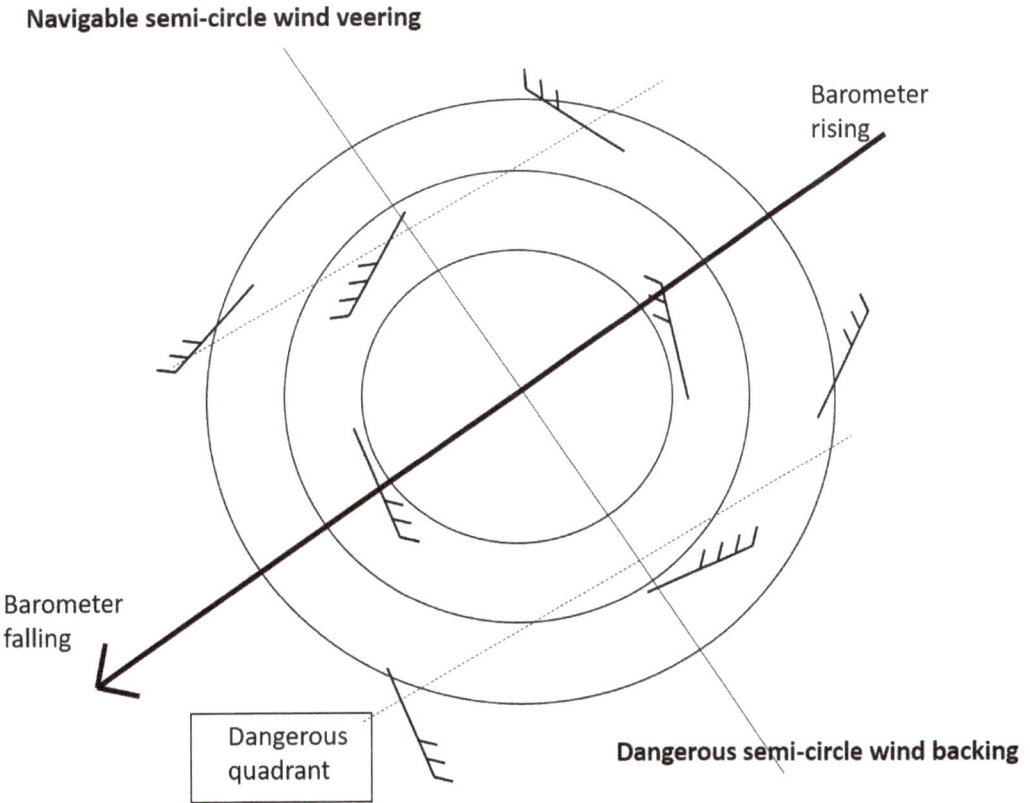

Storm Surge

Storm surge is a rising of the sea level as a result of wind and atmospheric pressure changes associated with a storm. The low atmospheric pressure allows the sea level to rise. The wind can be driven onshore, causing the water to be piled up or set-up along the coasts and in bays and harbours. By reducing the effectiveness of breakwaters, banks, and reefs as breakwaters, a storm surge may allow large waves into marinas and other safe heavens.

A storm surge is identified by its visual height measured above the normal predicted astronomical tide. The primary cause is the storm's wind pushing water onshore. The location (low-lying land), intensity of storm, size, speed all affect the height, as does the bathymetry (sea bed).

The highest storm tides are often observed during cyclones that coincide with a new or full moon.

Think of a surge as a raised dome of water that can be several metres higher than the usual tide level. Although it is difficult to quantify due to wind strength and topography.

Measuring the Strength of Tropical Revolving Storms, Cyclones, Hurricanes & Typhoons

The USA uses the Saffir-Simpson Hurricane Scale, but Australia uses a different scale for their cyclones, which are issued by BOM. Both have category one as the weakest wind speed, increasing up to category five (strongest wind speed).

Saffir-Simpson Scale

1. 74-95 mph   Minimal
2. 96-110 mph   Moderate
3. 111-130 mph   Major
4. 131-155 mph   Extensive
5. > 155 mph   Catastrophic

Australian Scale

1. 63-88 km/h
2. 89-117 km/h
3. 118-159 km/h Severe
4. 160-199 km/h Severe
5. > 200 km/h   Severe

To convert mph into km/h multiply by 1.6.
To convert km/h into mph divide by 1.6.

Whatever the distinction between cyclones, hurricanes, etc., being caught in one of these extraordinary systems would be a nightmare. If you want to cruise in the areas where these storms occur, carry out your research with books, the internet, local authorities for anchorage locations and have a plan. Read your insurance documentation carefully, as it may well state which latitudes you should avoid at specific times of the year. And remember that low-lying coastal areas will suffer with storm surges

Cyclone Warning System

The BOM supplies Tropical Cyclone Threat Maps and Warning Messages
http://www.bom.gov.au/cyclone/about/warnings/

Forecasting Weather

Weather Forecasts

You must remember that they are called weather 'forecasts' and they offer no guarantees. The weather usually determines when it is best to depart. It is imperative to understand marine forecasts and how to obtain forecasts for the area you are in. Weather can be a complex subject. It is beneficial to study as much weather forecasting theory as possible. And remember local factors influence the overall weather supplied by forecasters.

Australian has the most highly variable climate of all the continents. It is the most diverse from tropical to alpine.

It is generally agreed upon by forecasters that:
- A long period of wet weather is almost certain if the clouds appear in order: cirrus, alto cumulus, stratus and nimbus.
- The Cumulonimbus cloud is present in showery weather, particularly thunderstorms.
- Cumulus clouds are fine weather clouds. They develop during the day and, in the evening, they flatten out and are often coloured purple by the sun.

When to Listen to Forecasts
- Start getting an idea of what the weather is doing a week before departure.
- Pay particular attention two days leading up to departure.
- Check the weather before you leave, particularly the synoptic chart and the area west of you.
- En route, check the weather twice daily.
- If specific weather develops, (for example, a low), check the weather as often as possible.
- Monitor the weather at anchor and in a marina.

It is good practice to seek a wind/wave forecast for 24 and 48 hours, and synoptic charts (isobars and wind strength) for 24, 48 and 72 hours. The wind strength arrows can cover a large area.

Sources of Weather Information

As mariners, we must stay tuned into the weather at all time. Most coastal radio stations provide regular local weather forecasts on VHF radio, with instructions and broadcast times announced regularly on channel 16.

For more information, the Bureau of Meteorology and Australian Communications and Media Authority (ACMA) have produced a video on using VHF marine radio for weather information: https://www.youtube.com/watch?v=TssMnEZoO_E&feature=youtu.be

VHF Broadcasts by State and Territory Authorities

The marine transport and safety agencies of the State and Northern Territory governments are responsible for the dissemination of maritime safety information, including weather information, for small craft (under 300 tonnes) on VHF radio. Please refer to the relevant VHF operator in your State/Territory.

Full details: ACMA YouTube video (in collaboration with BOM):
https://www.youtube.com/watch?v=TssMnEZoO_E&feature=youtu.be

Your VHF radio is the best source for marine forecasts. You can also source weather via:
- Commercial radio
- Television
- Newspapers
- WeatherFax via SSB (HF) – worldwide
- VHF Radio Broadcasts by States and Territories:
  http://www.bom.gov.au/marine/radio-sat/marine-weather-vhf-radio.shtml
- High Frequency (HF) (SSB) Radio, BOM:
  http://www.bom.gov.au/marine/radio-sat/voice-services.shtml
- Other vessels

Charleville (VMC) Broadcast Schedule

Marine weather warnings are broadcast on the hour (on the half-hour in Central Standard Time (CST)) for NT, QLD, NSW, VIC, SA and TAS coastal waters zones and for all high seas areas. The broadcast is available on the following frequencies (kHz):

- Day-time (0700 – 1800 EST): 4426, 8176, 12365, 16546
- Night-time (1800 – 0700 EST): 2201, 6507, 8176, 12365

Navigation Maritime Safety Information notices are broadcast at 25 past each hour on 8176 kHz. Marine forecasts and observations are broadcast from Charleville (VMC) on a four-hour repeat cycle according to the schedule in the index.

WeatherFax

Become familiar with the WeatherFax process and schedule prior to departure. If you are in a marina, the signal may not work very well due to interference from masts and equipment.

To utilise WeatherFax all you need is a good SSB radio (HF), a laptop and an earphone connection from the radio to the laptop. Free software for downloading WeatherFax is available on the Internet.
http://www.jvcomm.de/index_e.html

Receiving weather via WeatherFax:
- You must deduct *1.9 kHz off the listed frequencies.
- To receive a good WeatherFax is easy, but the atmospherics can cause disturbances. Ensure you have done everything you can to receive a good picture.
- Turn off EVERYTHING:
  - the fridge

- wind generators
- solar panels
- inverters
- electronic steering gear (get someone to hand steer for a while or use the wind vane)
- all electrical devices
- solar panels (install a switch that lets you manually turn them off)

This can be done as a check procedure, one item at a time and note what items, if any, are causing interference.

*The deduction of 1.9kHz takes you to the carrier frequency of the transmission. Which means the transmission of a fixed frequency has been altered (modulated) to 'carry' data. We must simply adjust the published frequency by deducting 1.9kHz, however smaller adjustments (less than 1.9kHz) may provide a better picture.

Deciphering pictures: The synoptic charts are useful because they show you why the wind is doing what it is doing, and it can show you an escape route. You can clearly see what is coming.

Download the worldwide frequency list from:
http://www.nws.noaa.gov/om/marine/rfax.pdf

Remember:
- Subtract 1.9kHz from the given frequency.
- Some of the listed times are not exact and can change.
- Faxes can come a few minutes earlier and often later than the scheduled times.

Reading a Synoptic Chart

Synoptic Charts – Mean Sea Level Pressure Analysis (MSLP)

The synoptic information is compiled from hundreds of weather observations around Australia. To get a complete picture of the weather around the world, weather observations are taken at agreed times at weather stations worldwide. They are then plotted onto a synoptic chart.

They typically range in size from hundreds to thousands of kilometres across. Notably for the smooth, curving patterns of sea level isobars, these indicate lines of equal atmospheric pressure. These lines highlight the central elements of our weather systems: highs, lows, and cold fronts.

The synoptic chart is similar to a topographical chart where it shows the variation in atmospheric pressure over the Earth's surface.

We must remember that is a fairly simplistic representation of past, present, and future locations of weather systems, but it does provide an extremely useful guide.

Other obvious features are the patterns of high and low pressure and the barbed lines that identify cold fronts. The Earth's rotation causes air to flow clockwise around a low pressure system and anticlockwise around high pressure systems (this, of course, is in the southern hemisphere, the opposite occurs in the northern hemisphere).

As a reminder, friction over the Earth's surface cause the winds to be deflected inwards towards low pressure centres, and slightly outwards from high pressure systems.

The distance between the isobars is directly related to the wind strength, the closer the lines, the stronger the winds. (In the Tropics where the rotation is weaker, this does not apply, therefore in this area isobars are usually replaced with streamline arrows which indicate wind and direction without directly relating to pressure gradient).

Shaded areas show where rain has fallen in the last twenty-four hours. Wind direction is shown with arrows, the barbs indicate the speed (in the previous diagrams above).

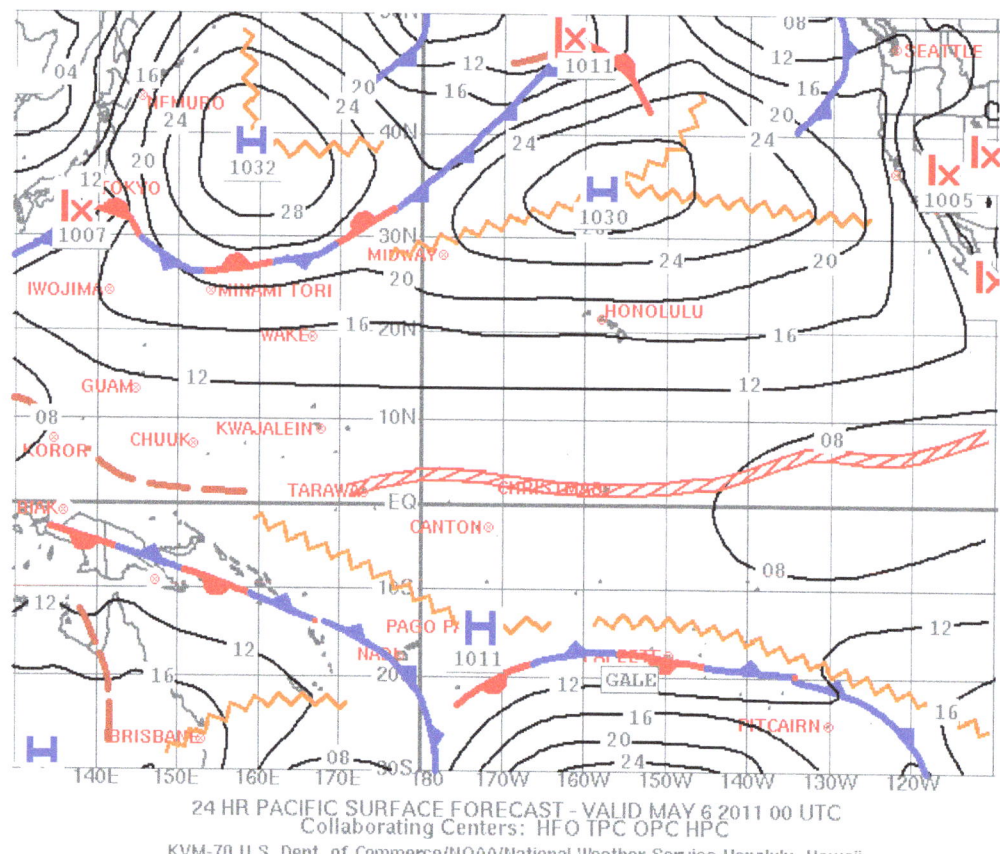

This is a sample of a synoptic chart from the National Oceanic and Atmospheric Administration (NOAA) in America. You can see the highs and the lows either side of the equator. The thick striped line near the equator is the ITZC (Intertropical Zone of Convergence). There is a large cold front (blue), heading for Pago Pago (American Samoa). The sawtooth line is a high pressure ridge. The dashed red line on the bottom left over Australia is a trough. All of these systems would and could provide strong winds, squalls and would provide you with a forewarning of unsettled weather.

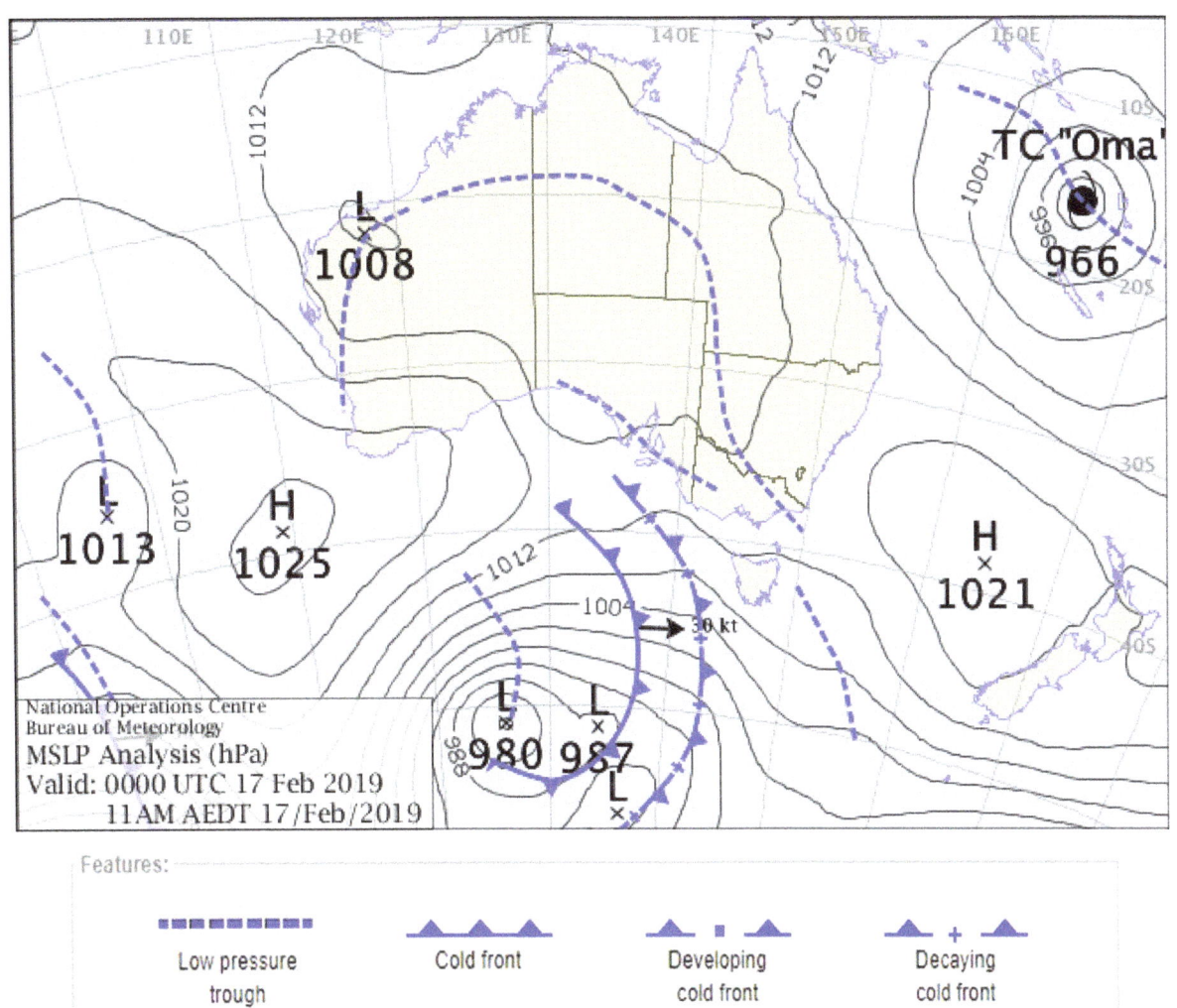

Reproduced by permission of Bureau of Meteorology, © 2018 Commonwealth of Australia

A range of highs and lows: A low pressure trough (part of low) is heading towards NZ, followed by two cold fronts and another low pressure trough.

Remembering that in the southern hemisphere air flows clockwise around low pressure systems and anticlockwise around high pressure systems, a fairly typical summer Australian weather map (below: Image One) shows:

You can see north to north-westerly winds over eastern Australia on the western side of a Tasman Sea high. They carry hot, dry air from inland Australia southward over Victoria and Tasmania. With strong winds associated with an approaching trough and cold front, this represents a classic weather situation with extreme bushfire risk.

The moist, easterly flow from the Coral Sea onto the Queensland coast causes very warm, humid and sultry weather east of the Great Dividing Range. This air, often susceptible to the development of showers and thunderstorms and is described as 'unstable'.

The cold front approaching Tasmania will replace the hot, dry north-westerlies with south-westerlies carrying cooler, often relatively humid air from waters south of the continent.

Such summer fronts are often quite shallow and may not penetrate far inland, particularly if they are distorted and slowed over the Victorian mountains.

Tropical Cyclone Freddy is moving offshore and the low heading for the Queensland coast is something to pay attention to, this time of year.

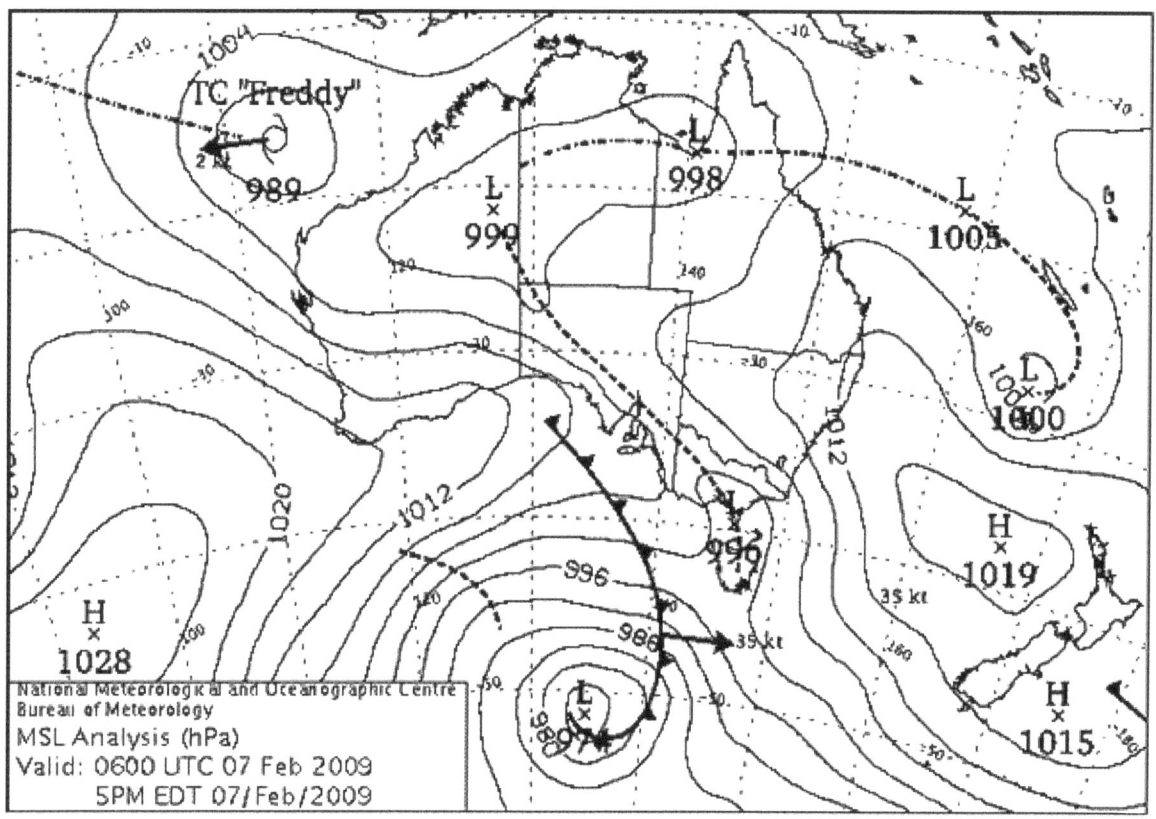

Image One: A common Australian summer weather map
Reproduced by permission of Bureau of Meteorology, © 2018 Commonwealth of Australia

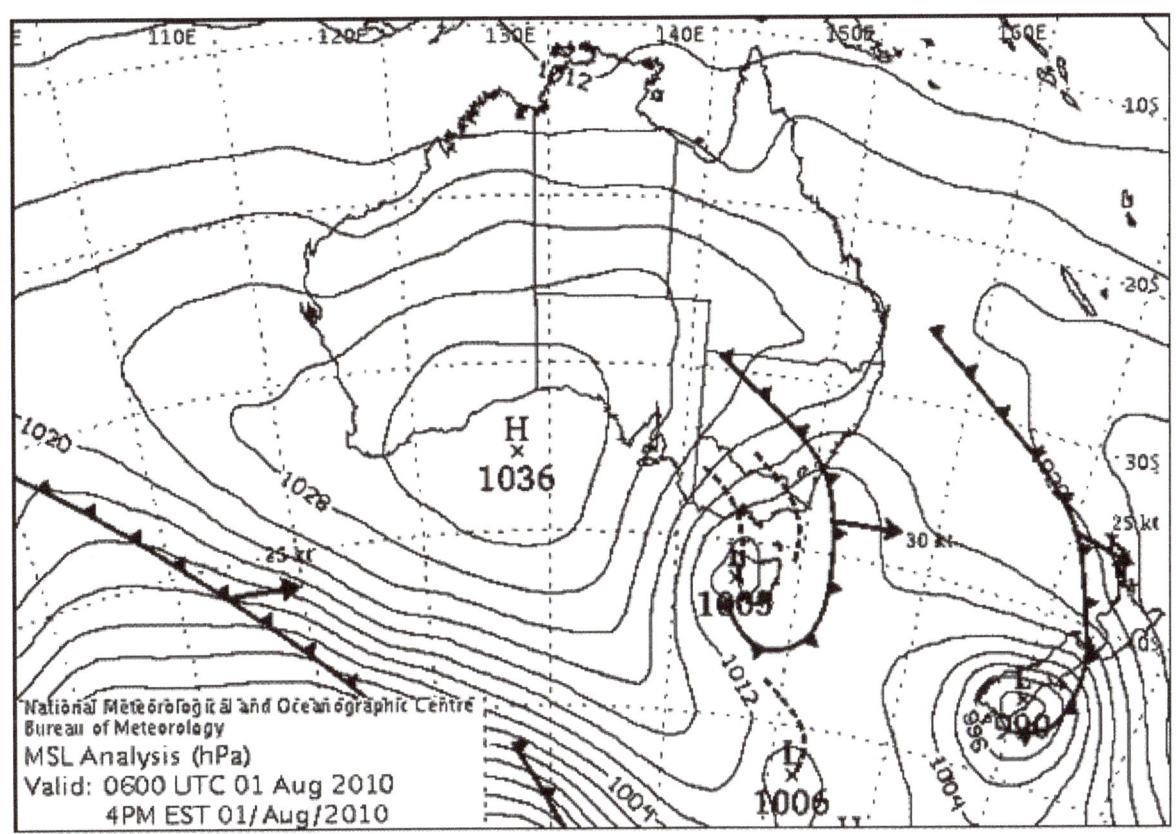
Image Two: a common winter weather map.
Reproduced by permission of Bureau of Meteorology, © 2018 Commonwealth of Australia

Very cold, unstable air from well south of Tasmania is flowing northward over Tasmania, Victoria and southeast New South Wales, reducing normal day temperatures typically by five degrees or more. Note the cold front, the low centred over Tasmania and the South Island of New Zealand, and the high (1036 hectopascals) over the Bight. Occasionally, rapid interaction with other weather systems can almost halt the pattern's eastward movement, causing successive cold fronts to bring a prolonged spell of cold, showery weather to southern Australia.

Easterly winds (i.e. blowing from the east) over (northern) inland Australia: Although southern Cold Fronts become shallow and diffuse as they move into northern Australia they often trigger a surge in the strength of the easterlies and this, combined with their extreme dryness, creates a very high fire danger in the tropical savanna region.

Rain or Fine?

Features on the surface weather chart indicate likely rainfall patterns as well as temperature distribution and wind strength. In general, highs tend to be associated with subsiding (sinking) air and generally fine weather, while lows are associated with ascending (rising) air and usually produce rain or showers.

While cloud can exist without rain, the opposite is not the case.

Clouds form as water vapour condenses as it cools. Causes of cooling include:

Convection: The transfer of thermal energy in air or water. Warm air is less dense and rises, colder air is denser and sinks causing a circular motion. It may be initiated by warming of low-level air, forced ascent over mountainous country, or dynamic causes associated with severe weather systems. Cumulus clouds often form as a result of convection. The most exceptional forms are often associated with severe thunderstorms and occasionally, tornados. Cumulonimbus, for instance, may reach altitudes above 15,000 metres.

Systematic Ascent of Moist Air: A systematic ascent of moist air over large areas is linked with large-scale weather systems such as low pressure systems, including tropical cyclones. In mid-latitudes, this systematic ascent often occurs ahead of active fronts, or with cut off lows. This type of rain may be persistent and heavy and cause floods, especially if enhanced by forced (orographic) ascent over mountains.

Orographic Ascent: Orographic ascent occurs when air is forced upwards by a barrier of mountains or hills. Cloud formation and rainfall is often the result. Australia's heaviest rainfall occurs on the Queensland coast and in western Tasmania, where prevailing maritime airstreams are forced to lift over mountain ranges.

Cold and Warm Fronts: Cold and warm fronts also cause systematic ascent. A cold front is the boundary where cold air moves to replace, and undercut, warmer and less dense air. Associated cloud and weather may vary enormously according to the properties of the air masses, but tends to be concentrated near the front. As a cold front approaches winds freshen from the north or northwest, and pressure falls. After the front passes, winds shift direction anticlockwise ('backing' to the west or southwest) and pressure rises. Cold fronts are much more frequent and vigorous over southern Australia than elsewhere. Warm fronts, relatively infrequent over Australia, are usually found in high latitudes where they can occasionally cause significant weather. They are often shown on weather charts over the Southern Ocean. Warm fronts progressively displace cool air by warmer air.

Convergence Lifting: Convergence lifting occurs when more air flows into an area at low levels than flows out, leading to forced rising of large air masses. Convergence is often associated with wave-like disturbances in tropical easterlies and may also occur with broad tropical air masses flowing to the south. Given sufficient atmospheric moisture and instability, it may cause large cloud clusters and rain.

How Strong Will the Winds Be?

A mean sea level pressure chart shows the direct relationship between isobar spacing (pressure gradient) and orientation, and the strength and direction of surface winds. The general rule is that winds are strongest where the isobars are closest together. Thus, the strongest winds are usually experienced near cold fronts, low pressure systems and in westerly airstreams south of the continent. Winds are normally light near high pressure systems where the isobars are widely spaced.

However, because of a latitude effect (the Coriolis Effect) winds in middle latitudes are lighter than those in the tropics with similarly spaced isobars.

In Australia, the most destructive winds over broad areas are generated by tropical cyclones. (Tornados, associated with some severe thunderstorms, have the potential to generate higher wind speeds, but areas affected are much smaller than these tropical storms.)

Tropical cyclones are low pressure systems in the tropics which, in the southern hemisphere, have well-defined clockwise circulations with mean surface winds (averaged over ten minutes) exceeding gale force (63 kilometres per hour) surrounding the centre. Tropical cyclones exhibit a relatively clear eye, surrounded by dense wall clouds and a series of spiral rain-bands. The BOM tracks cyclones with weather watch radar, special service reports and frequent satellite images. The image below shows a tropical cyclone approaching, and crossing the Queensland coast near Rockhampton.

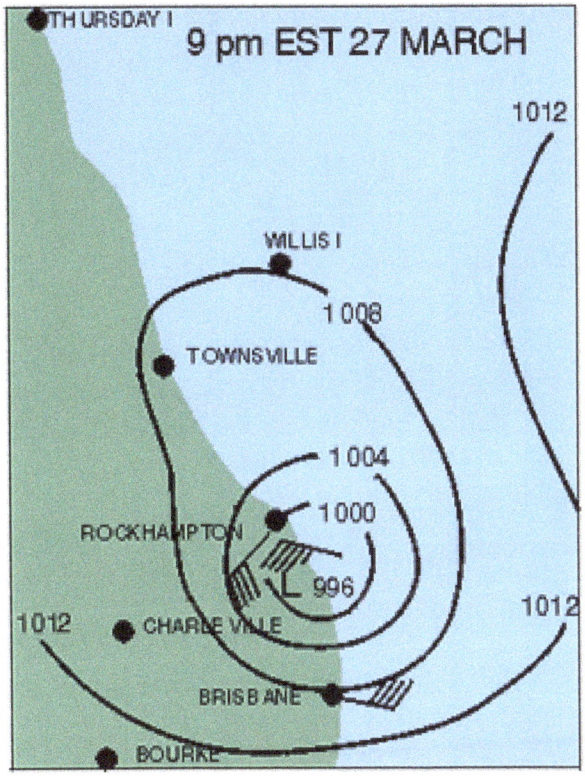

The image above shows a chart of a cyclone moving from the Coral Sea to the Queensland coast demonstrating how isobars indicate wind speed and direction.
Reproduced by permission of Bureau of Meteorology, © 2018 Commonwealth of Australia

The pressure gradient is very steep towards the cyclone's centre with great wind speeds.

Wind maps that forecast the wind will either be shaded to show the speed of the wind (with small arrows indicating direction) or each arrow will indicate direction with feathers. Each feather is 10 knots, half a feather is 5 knots. (Cyclone danger-zone diagrams later in this manual show the weather arrows with feathers).

Line Squalls

A line squall is an extremely active or severe cold front. This is where the temperature difference between the cold air and warm air is large and the warm air mass is extremely unstable. Convection along the front is massive. Line squalls are sometimes not forecast because the front intensifies during its passage. Any cold front, especially a sharp one, must be viewed with caution and a closer weather watch adhered to.

Sailing the Pacific Ocean on Mariah II. We relied on WeatherFax for our forecasts.
We knew this was coming a long time before we saw it in the sky.

Often a long low black rolling cloud stretches across the horizon in advance of a front that accompanies the line squall. The cloud is caused by the rapid advance of the cold sector forcing the air in the warm sector at the front to be tumbled over. The warm air, being close to saturation, condenses out.

Often, line squalls occur ahead of a front and can rapidly form as isolated systems. The weather associated with these is often severe and dangerous if not anticipated.

Col

A Col is the region between two highs and two lows that are diagonally opposed. Generally light, variable winds occur near the centre of a col. Fog may occur, particularly in autumn and winter.

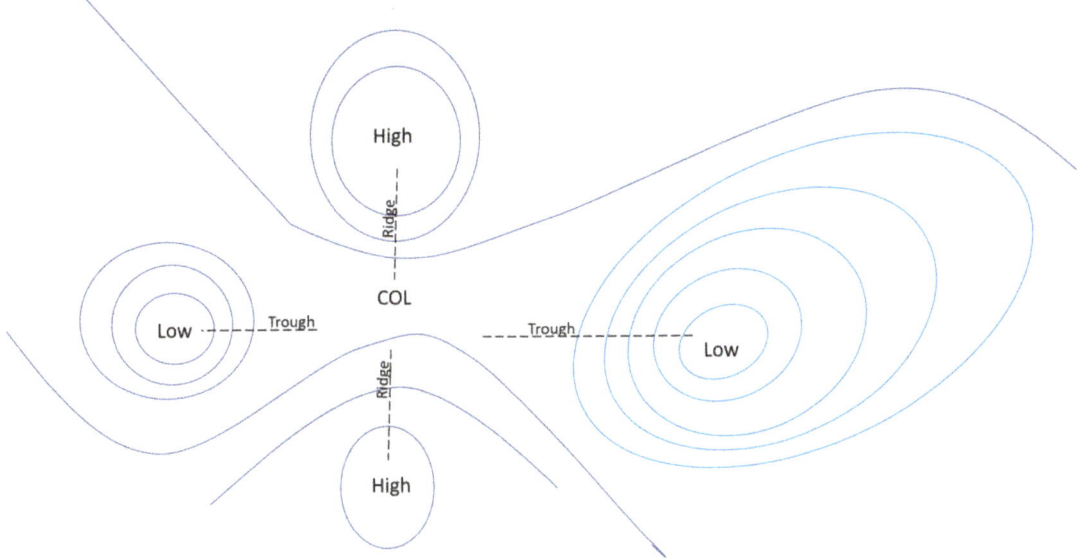

A Case Study

The diagrams below show the projected atmospheric conditions over four days.

Remember, in summer, low pressure systems dominate northern Australia, bringing the wet season. For the southern part of Australia, high pressure systems dominate with the occasional passage of a cold front that moves from west to east. These sometimes travel up the southeast coast, often accompanied by frontal thunderstorms.

In winter, the high pressure systems migrate to the north, bringing stable atmospheric conditions and a dry winter to the north of Australia. The low pressure systems, which travel to the south of the continent in summer, also move to the north, bringing unsettled conditions to the southern part of Australia.

The following pictures are typical of the Australian winter. Maps are prepared by the BOM for 1000 and for 2200.

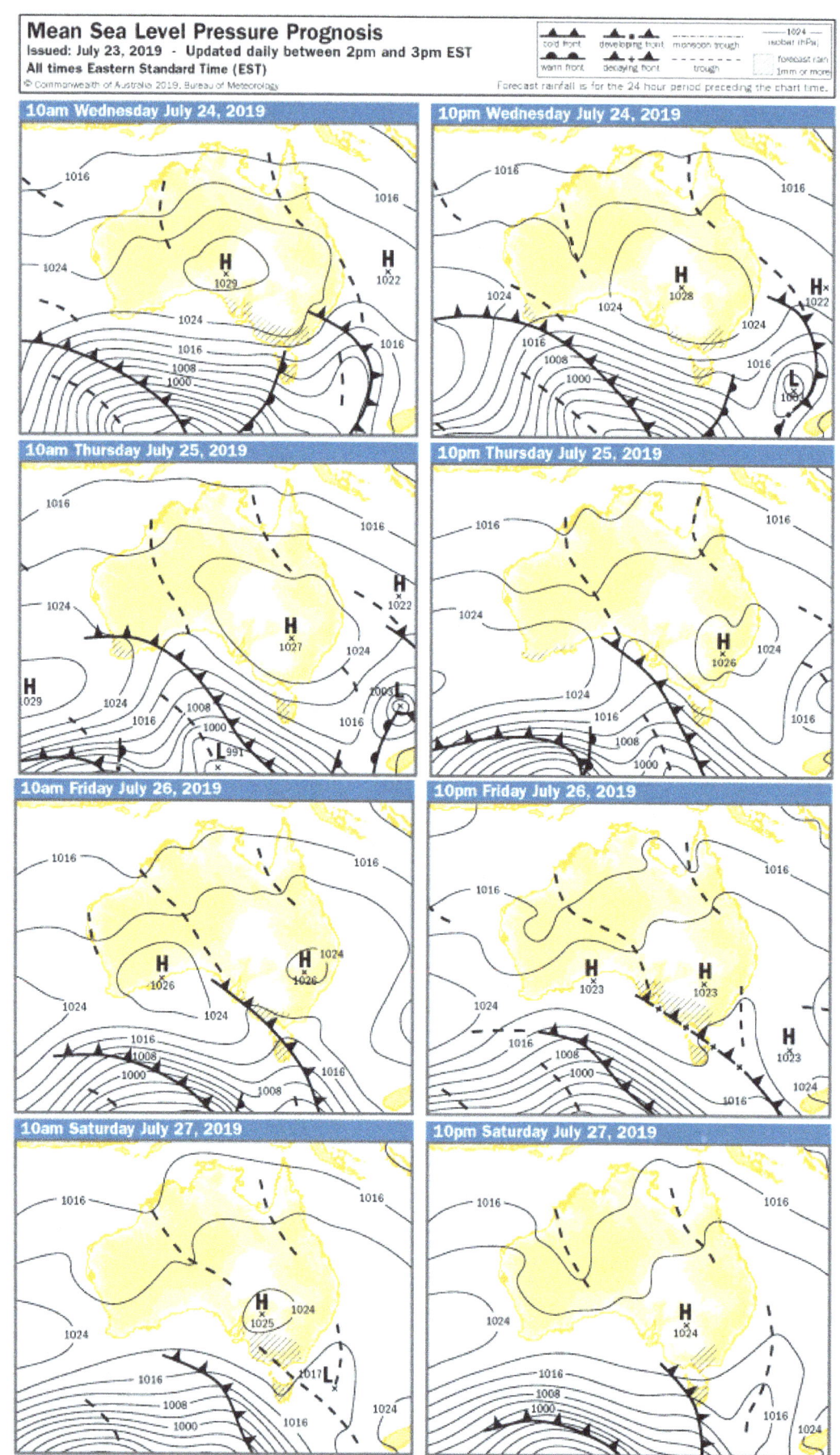

Reproduced by permission of Bureau of Meteorology, © 2018 Commonwealth of Australia

Buys Ballot's Law

BUYS BALLOT'S LAW determines the approximate direction of the centre of a low or a high pressure system.

In the southern hemisphere, face the wind and the centre of the low pressure will lie between 90 and 135 degrees on your left-hand side, (this does depend on your distance from the centre of the storm). When the pressure begins to fall, the centre is about (135°). When it has fallen 10 hPa the centre is at about 10 points (112.5°). And when it has fallen 20 hPa the centre is at about 8 points (90°). Reverse this rule for the high pressure [and for the northern hemisphere].

Forecasting Exercise

EXERCISE – STUDY SYNOPTIC CHARTS

Wind
1. Identify the wind direction and strength by looking at the isobars adjacent to your area.
2. Identify the circulation and direction.
3. Check the angle of indraft

Interpret wind direction
The wind strength depends on the pressure gradient, that is, isobars close, stronger wind isobars wide apart, light winds.

Remember, wind is also influenced by local sea breeze.

Associated Weather
Identify the source of the air mass affecting your area, refer to highs and lows, troughs and ridges. This will indicate the specific characteristics and enable you to identify an associated weather.

Sea State
Is directly dependent on the wind strength, refer to the Beaufort Scale.

Swell
Study the previous synoptic charts and identify the duration and direction in which the swell has been generating.

Outlook
This is the prognosis of what is going to happen beyond the next twenty-four-hours. You will need to refer to the previous synoptic charts and anticipate the most likely movement of the systems. Then using the above guidelines produce the outlook.

> **Comfort at Sea**
> **Wet Weather Gear**
> Good quality wet weather gear is imperative if you want to avoid being miserable while sailing in rain. When buying new gear, buy one size too big and/or try it on with many layers of clothes. Most use will occur when it is cold as well as raining. You will want to be able to sail the boat and move around with the gear on. That won't be possible if it is too tight.
>
> We like gear with velcro around the ankles and wrists, it doesn't keep all the rain out, but certainly helps. Breathable gear is important too. Some brands have an inbuilt harness; these may not be tight enough, especially if you have purchased a larger jacket to be able to wear all your clothes beneath it. We prefer separate harnesses that incorporate a life jacket.
>
> You can buy different coloured gear and we always wonder why they sell blue and white. The idea is to be seen: go for red, orange or fluoro green/yellow with reflectors sewn in. Aside from heavy duty wet weather gear, we have lighter jackets for short showers in warm weather. Once in port, wash the used gear in fresh water and dry it properly prior to stowing.

BUREAU OF METEOROLOGY SERVICES

BOM Tropical cyclone services
The BOM provides a range of tropical cyclone related advice.

Tropical cyclone seasonal outlook Issued at the beginning of the season to provide an estimate of the level of tropical cyclone activity in the coming season.

Tropical cyclone outlook Issued daily throughout the tropical cyclone season. They provide a forecast of the probability of cyclone development in the seas around Australia.

Tropical cyclone information bulletin Issued when a cyclone is active in the Australian region, but is not expected to impact land-based communities within 48 hours.

Tropical cyclone watch Issued if a cyclone is expected to affect coastal communities within 48 hours, but not expected within twenty-four-hours.

Tropical cyclone warning Issued if a cyclone is affecting or is expected to affect coastal communities within twenty-four-hours.

Technical bulletin The *Tropical Cyclone Technical Bulletin* provides technical details about the cyclone.

Tropical cyclone forecast track map Issued with tropical cyclone advices to give a graphical representation of the cyclone's past track forecast movement and its threat area.

Tropical cyclone forecast track maps: GIS Compatible Format All current forecast map graphics available in GIS compatible format. (A GIS file format is a standard of encoding geographical information into a computer file.) These maps are created mainly by government mapping agencies, allowing technicians to share and create data in various geospatial data formats.

Marine warnings Marine warnings are issued for high seas and coastal waters threatened by cyclones.

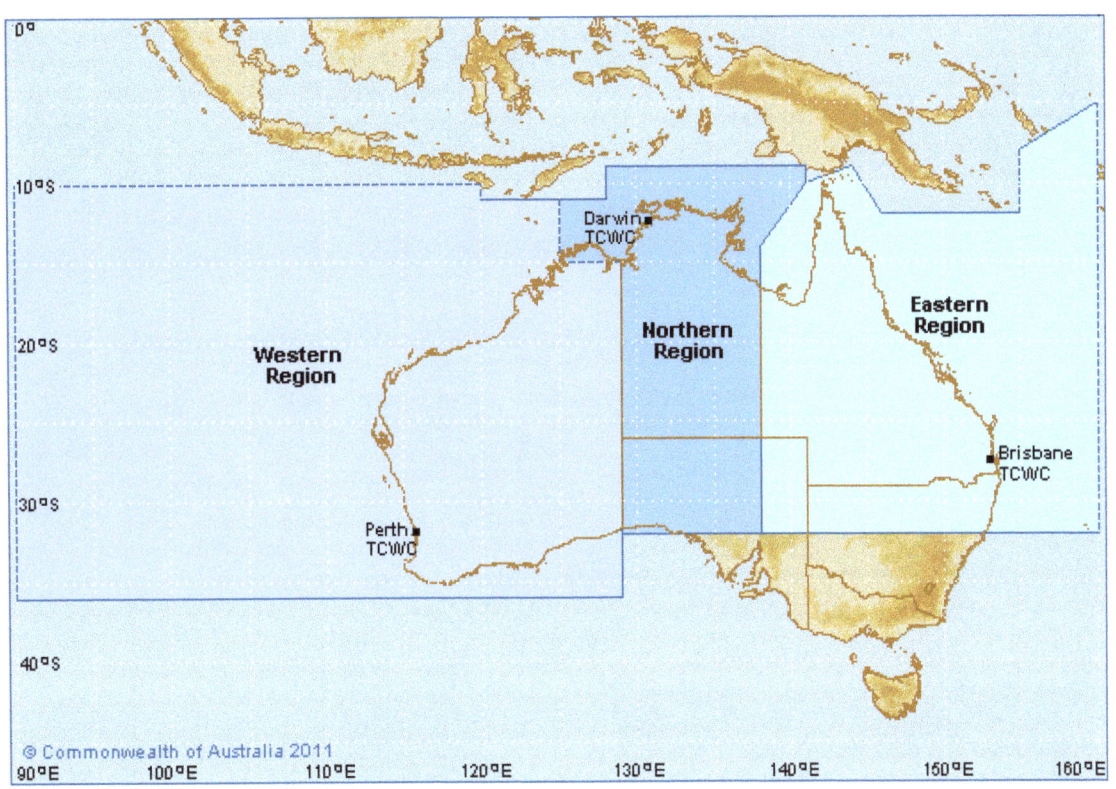

http://www.bom.gov.au/cyclone/
Reproduced by permission of Bureau of Meteorology, © 2018 Commonwealth of Australia

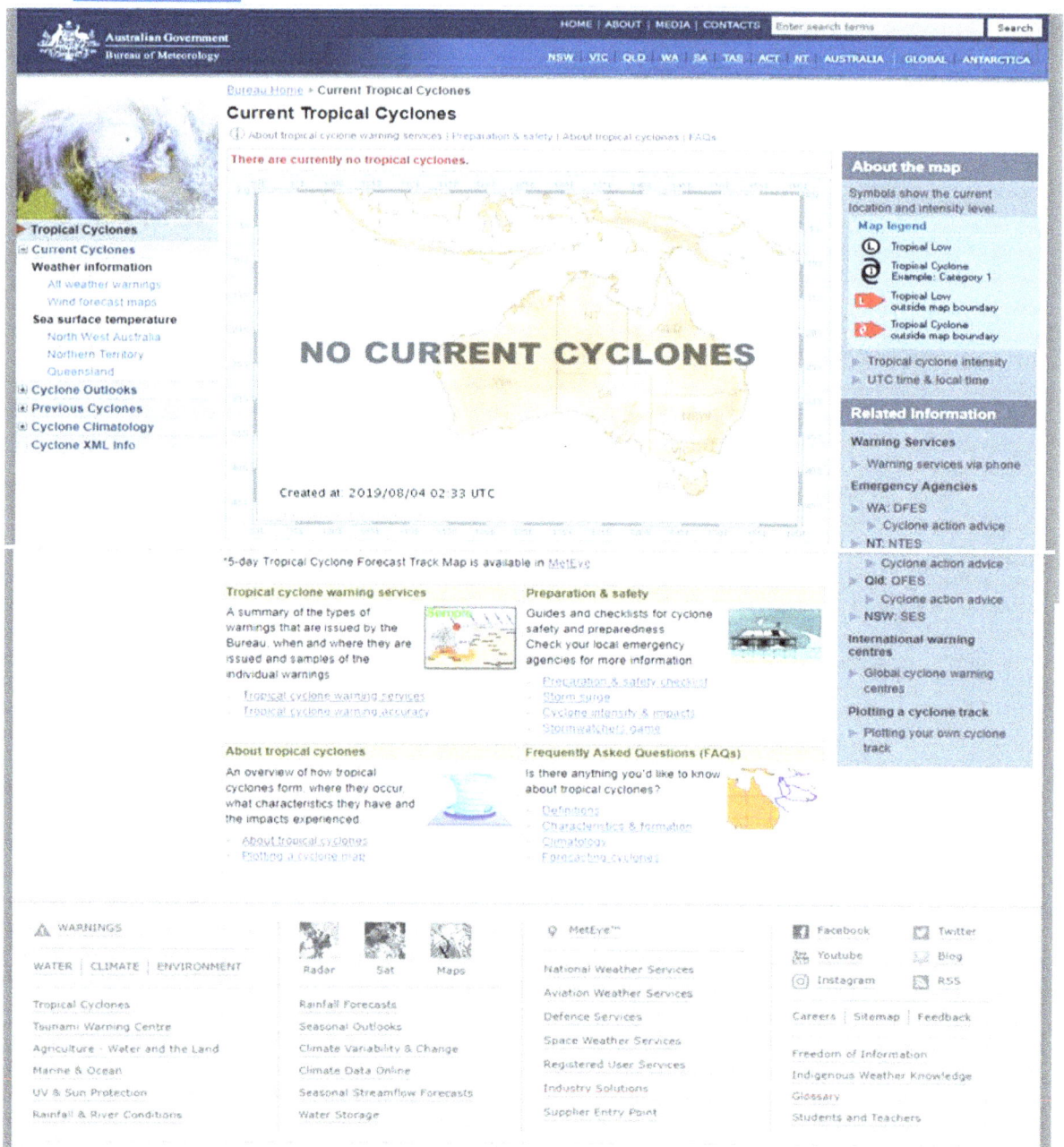

Reproduced by permission of Bureau of Meteorology, © 2018 Commonwealth of Australia

HF Radio Stations from BOM

The BOM broadcasts marine weather warnings, forecasts, and observations via HF radio to assist mariners travelling offshore.

The **Charleville transmitters (VMC – Australia Weather East)** broadcast weather information for Australia's eastern waters. The VMC voice schedule is as follows:

(Correct at the time of publishing – you can update/check the schedules here: http://www.bom.gov.au/marine/radio-sat/voice-services.shtml)

Weather bulletin	EST*	CST*	WST	UTC	Frequencies (kHz)
Coastal Waters forecasts for Queensland	0730	0700	0530	2130	4426
	1130	1100	0930	0130	8176
	1530	1500	1330	0530	12365
					16546
	1930	1900	1730	0930	2201
	2330	2300	2130	1330	6507
	0330	0300	0130	1730	8176
					12365
Coastal Waters forecasts for New South Wales and Victoria	0930	0900	0730	2330	4426
	1330	1300	1130	0330	8176
	1730	1700	1530	0730	12365
					16546
	2130	2100	1930	1130	2201
	0130	0100	2330	1530	6507
	0530	0500	0330	1930	8176
					12365
Coastal Waters forecasts for Tasmania	1030	1000	0830	0030	4426
					8176
	1430	1400	1230	0430	12365
					16546
	1830	1800	1630	0830	2201
	2230	2200	2030	1230	6507
	0230	0200	0030	1630	8176
	0630	0600	0430	2030	12365
High Seas forecasts for Northern, North-Eastern, South-Eastern, and Southern areas	0830	0800	0630	2230	4426
	1230	1200	1030	0230	8176
	1630	1600	1430	0630	12365
					16546
	2030	2000	1830	1030	2201
	0030	0000	2230	1430	6507
	0430	0400	0230	1830	8176
					12365
Marine weather warnings are broadcast on the hour (on the half-hour in CST) for NT, QLD NSW, VIC SA, and TAS coastal waters zones and for all high seas areas.					
Navigation maritime safety information notices are broadcast at 25 past each hour.					

Notes
- Coastal Waters forecasts are for areas within 60 nautical miles of the coast
- EST = Australian Eastern Standard Time   WST = Australian Western Standard Time
- CST = Australian Central Standard Time   UTC = Coordinated Universal Time
  *During daylight saving time, add 1 hour to EST and CST to obtain AEDT and ACDT equivalent.

The **Wiluna transmitters (VMW – Australia Weather West)** broadcast weather information for Australia's western waters. The VMW voice schedule is as follows:

Weather bulletin	WST*	CST*	EST*	UTC	Frequencies (kHz)
Coastal Waters forecasts for: • Western Australia (Northern Zones: NT–WA Border to North-West Cape) • Northern Territory	0730 1130 1530	0900 1300 1700	0930 1330 1730	2330 0330 0730	4149 8113 12362 16528
	1930 2330 0330	2100 0100 0500	2130 0130 0530	1130 1530 1930	2056 6230 8113 12362
Coastal Waters forecasts for: • Western Australia (Western Zones: North-West Cape to Cape Naturaliste) • Western Australia (Southern Zones: Cape Naturaliste to WA–SA Border)	0830 1230 1630	1000 1400 1800	1030 1430 1830	0030 0430 0830	4149 8113 12362 16528
	2030 0030 0430	2200 0200 0600	2230 0230 0630	1230 1630 2030	2056 6230 8113 12362
Coastal Waters forecasts for South Australia	0930 1330 1730	1100 1500 1900	1130 1530 1930	0130 0530 0930	4149 8113 12362 16528
	2130 0130 0530	2300 0300 0700	2330 0330 0730	1330 1730 2130	2056 6230 8113 12362
Coastal Waters forecasts for Queensland (Gulf waters)	1030 1430	1200 1600	1230 1630	0230 0630	4149 8113 12362 16528
High Seas forecasts for Northern, Western, and Southern areas	1830 2230 0230	2000 0000 0400	2030 0030 0430	1030 1430 1830	2056 6230 8113 12362
	0630	0800	0830	2230	
Marine weather warnings are broadcast on the hour (on the half-hour in CST) for Qld Gulf, NT, WA and SA coastal waters zones and for all high seas areas.					
Navigation maritime safety information notices are broadcast at 25 past each hour.					

Notes

- Coastal Waters forecasts are for areas within 60 nautical miles of the coast
- WST = Australian Western Standard Time EST = Australian Eastern Standard Time
- CST = Australian Central Standard Time UTC = Coordinated Universal Time
    * During daylight saving time, add 1 hour to EST and CST to obtain AEDT and ACDT equivalent

    (Last updated February 2019. Please check www.bom.gov.au/marine for the latest schedule)

Telephone Weather Services Directory

Telephone Weather Services Directory

User Guide | Directory last updated January 2016

Telephone Weather Services Call Charges

- 1900 numbers: 77c per minute incl. GST
- 1300 numbers: Low call cost - around 27.5c incl. GST
- 1196 numbers: Low call cost - around 27.5c incl. GST

(More from international, mobile or public phones)

Please Note: Bureau of Meteorology Telephone Weather Services (TWS) deliver pre-recorded messages only. Contact us for alternative delivery options.

Select your Region

WA	NT	SA	QLD	NSW	ACT	VIC	TAS

Service	Phone Number
National	
National Telephone Weather Services Directory	1900 926 113
National Telephone Weather Service	1900 955 369
National Marine Service	1900 955 370
Australian Capital City Brief Forecasts	1900 926 161
Australian Seasonal Outlook Summary (3 Months)	1900 926 162
Australian Tsunami Threat Information (1300 TSUNAMI)	**1300 878 6264**
National Weather Warnings	1300 659 210

New South Wales	
Full State Service	1900 955 361
Sydney Metropolitan Service	1900 926 100
Sydney Waters Service	1900 969 955
Sydney Metropolitan Temperature and Weather Observations Service	1900 926 122
NSW Coastal Waters Service	1900 926 101
NSW Country Service	1900 926 102
Newcastle and Hunter Service	1900 969 954
Australian Tsunami Threat Information (1300 TSUNAMI)	*1300 878 6264*

Top

Victoria	
Full State Service	1900 955 363
Melbourne Metropolitan Service	1900 926 109
Melbourne Metropolitan Temperature and Weather Observations Service	1900 926 121
Port Phillip and Western Port: Local Waters Service	1900 926 110
Victoria: Coastal Waters Service	1900 969 930
Central Coast, Cape Otway to Wilsons Promontory: Coastal Waters Service	1900 969 931
Northern Tasmania: Coastal Waters Service	1900 969 932
East Coast, Wilsons Promontory to 60nm east of Gabo Island: Coastal Waters Service	1900 969 933
West Coast, SA/VIC border to Cape Otway: Coastal Waters Service	1900 969 934
Victoria: Coastal and Local Waters Service	1900 969 966
VIC Country Service	1900 926 111
Yacht Forecast for Port Phillip and Western Port	1900 920 557
Australian Tsunami Threat Information (1300 TSUNAMI)	*1300 878 6264*

Queensland	
Full State Service	1900 955 360
Brisbane Metropolitan Service	1900 926 114
Brisbane Metropolitan Temperature Service	1900 926 123
QLD Coastal Waters Service	1900 969 923
QLD General Warnings	1900 969 922
Australian Tsunami Threat Information (1300 TSUNAMI)	*1300 878 6264*
Separate Regional Forecasts for Country Queensland	
QLD Northern Districts Service	1900 969 925
QLD Central Districts Service	1900 969 926
QLD Western Districts Service	1900 969 927
QLD Southeast Districts Service (except Southeast Coast)	1900 969 928
QLD Southeast Coast Service	1900 969 929
Southeast Queensland Boating Weather Service	1900 926 115

Western Australia	
Full State Service	1900 955 366
Perth Metropolitan Service	1900 926 149
Perth Metropolitan Temperature and Weather Observations Service	1900 926 119
Perth Local Waters Service	1900 955 350
WA Marine Service	1900 926 150
Northern WA Coastal Waters Service	1900 969 901
Western WA Coastal Waters Service	1900 969 902
Southern WA Coastal Waters Service	1900 969 903
WA Country Northern and Eastern Service	1900 969 904
WA Country Southwest Land Division Service	1900 969 905
WA General Warnings Service	1900 955 371
Australian Tsunami Threat Information (1300 TSUNAMI)	*1300 878 6264*

Top

South Australia	
Full State Service	1900 955 365
Adelaide Metropolitan Service	1900 926 144
Adelaide Metropolitan Temperature and Weather Observations Service	1900 926 120
SA Coastal Waters Service	1900 969 975
SA Country Service	1900 926 189
Australian Tsunami Threat Information (1300 TSUNAMI)	*1300 878 6264*

Tasmania	
TAS State, Cities and Districts Forecast Service	1900 955 364
TAS Boating Weather Service	1900 969 940
Hobart Temperature Service	1900 926 125
Australian Tsunami Threat Information (1300 TSUNAMI)	*1300 878 6264*

Top

Australian Capital Territory	
ACT Service	1900 955 362
NSW Illawarra and South Coast Service	1900 969 900
NSW Southern Inland Service	1900 969 906
Canberra Temperature and Weather Observations Service	1900 926 126

Top

Northern Territory	
Northern Territory Service	1900 955 367
Darwin Temperature and Weather Observations Service	1900 926 124
Australian Tsunami Threat Information (1300 TSUNAMI)	*1300 878 6264*

Telstra 1196 Weather Services

What 1196 services provide
Each Telstra 1196 Weather Service provides the current temperature, a list of current severe weather warnings and a 1-2 day forecast for a single population centre. All information originates from the Bureau of Meteorology and is provided through the service provider Legion Interactive.

SUMMARY

Congratulations, you've learned some basic weather safety measures in bad weather and studied synoptic charts. You are beginning to understand weather and these notes and tips are good preparation before taking a voyage, as part of passage planning.

APPENDIX 1: Cyclone Preparation

Obtain weather forecasts and track the storm's position and movement. Try not to rely on one source of information. Wear a life jacket and issue one to all on board, making sure they put them on. Work out the best track to sail (the safe/dangerous semicircle – see below). Get some sleep before the storm arrives, if you can.

Anchoring or in a Marina:
- Are there good hurricane holes that are reachable quickly? Is there enough room? You won't be the only boat there.
- Keep topped up with fuel and water.
- On a warning, proceed to your selected hurricane hole early.
- Does your boat insurance cover damage you may do to other boats? Think about boats in the same hurricane hole or next to you in a marina, will they be covered for damage they may inflict on you?
- Take pictures of your boat and all the expensive equipment and keep these pictures with your insurance policy in a safe place like your grab bag.
- Prior to the hurricane season starting, find out where to get information.

When a Cyclone Warning is Issued
- Prepare for the worst.
- If you have time, strip the exterior of your boat: sails*, dodger, canvas awnings, solar panels, wind generators, lines, BBQs, anchors and as many nonpermanent items you can. (*You may need your main, so leave it on, but lash it down very securely.)
- Stow your dinghy and outboards below.
- Tie, lash and fix everything else left outside.
- Ensure all lines (snubbers on anchor or lines in a marina) have spring (elasticity) in them. Rig up additional lines.
- Use rags, pipes, leather or foam on all possible chafing points.
- If you are on anchor and have time, dive on your anchor and check its setting. Ask other boats to do the same.
- If you are leaving your boat, remove all your personal items, specifically your personal and boat documentation and let someone know where you are.
- Turn on your navigation lights.
- Note your position in your log and on your chart.
- Let someone else know where you are, preferably someone onshore.
- Prepare several meals and hot liquids in a flask/thermos.
- Eat and feed everyone on board a hot meal.
- Get as much sleep as possible.
- Hand out seasickness pills (take them prior to the storm, you are going to experience horrendous conditions; it is better to be ready for becoming seasick, even if you have never suffered previously).
- Check every corner to ensure everything is stowed properly down below.

Personal Preparation
- Take seasickness medication early.
- Have torches and head lamps ready.
- Have snorkel gear (dive goggles) ready for going outside if necessary.
- Have wet weather gear and harnesses easily accessible.

Detailed Preparation

Above Decks:
- Remove/lash down anything loose, stowing below is best.
- Remove the anchor and chain and secure in a low spot below deck.
- Lash the spinnaker pole.
- Secure spare halyards.
- Prepare storm sails.
- Turn off the wind generator, lash down the blades or remove them.
- Check the self-steering gear, vane and paddle.
- Secure all vents.
- Remove winch handles from mast.
- Fit storm boards on portholes.
- Ensure propane tanks are secure using additional lashing.
- If you have an inflatable dinghy on deck, deflate and store below.
- Additional lashings on hard dinghy.
- Remove all sails and lines where possible and stow below.
- Find extra lines to tie down solar panels; in extreme conditions, you may consider cutting the wires and taking panels below.
- Stow jerry cans below where possible.
- Ensure swim ladder is in.

Cockpit:
- Remove anything loose.
- Remove biminis/dodgers and any canvas where possible.

Below decks:
- Ensure all hatches are closed and dogged firmly.
- Stow any loose items.
- Have extra bungs and hammer at the ready.
- Lock all lockers and drawers and oven door.
- Go through the entire boat, checking everything is secure.
- Rig up your lee cloths with additional lines to help keep you in the bunk.
- Double check your grab bag. (See 'Grab/Ditch Bag' in the Boat Equipment section.)
- Lash your full water jerry cans together in readiness in case you abandon ship (they will float, saltwater is denser than fresh).
- Review life-raft procedure and check all emergency equipment, flares etc.
- Clear navigation station of all plotting instruments.
- Test all bilge pumps.
- Test radios, if possible.
- Move heavy objects to the lowest part of your vessel and lash.

- Remove any food wanted before covering cupboards with sails and other equipment stowed below.
- Stow computer away properly and all other equipment.

Safety
- If you are on board and dragging towards shore and cannot stop it, try to stay on board for as long as possible.
- If you hit the shore, try and step ashore if it is safe to do so. Take your grab bag, which will hold all your documentation. This is obviously dependent on conditions, as it may be too dangerous to try.

Storm Surge
- You may not be in the full force of the storm, but storm surge can be felt hundreds of miles away.
- In a marina, double up your lines and ensure they have elasticity.

Remember: whatever preparation you have done and however smart you are, what about the person anchored just in front of you? Can you be sure that he has done the same amount of preparation?

GLOSSARY

AIR DENSITY The mass of air per unit volume.

AIR MASS An extensive body of air with approximately uniform temperature and moisture characteristics.

ALTOCUMULUS A principal cloud type, forming in the middle levels of the troposphere, and appearing as a white and/or grey layer or patch with a waved aspect.

ALTOSTRATUS A principal cloud type, forming in the middle levels of the troposphere, and appearing as a grey or bluish sheet.

ANABATIC WIND An uphill wind generated by the heating of a sloping surface.

ANEMOMETER An instrument used to measure wind speed and direction.

ANEROID BAROMETER A nonliquid instrument used to measure atmospheric pressure.

ANOMALOUS PROPAGATION The nonstandard propagation of a beam of energy (radio or radar) under certain atmospheric conditions, which results in false echoes (i.e. non-precipitation) on a radar image. Usually caused by unusual rates of refraction in the atmosphere.

ANTICYCLONE An extensive horizontal spiral movement of the atmosphere around and away from a central region of high pressure. The spiral motion is anticlockwise in the southern hemisphere and clockwise in the northern hemisphere.

ANVIL The upper portion of a Cumulonimbus cloud that spreads out under the tropopause, often in the shape of a blacksmith's anvil, sometimes for hundreds of kilometres downstream from the parent cloud. It indicates the mature or decaying stage of a thunderstorm.

ATMOSPHERE The gaseous portion of the physical environment that encircles the Earth. The divisions of the atmosphere are the troposphere, the stratosphere, the mesosphere, the ionosphere, and the exosphere.

ATMOSPHERIC PRESSURE The total weight of the atmosphere above the point of measurement.

BACKING A counterclockwise shift in the wind direction.

BAROMETER An instrument for measuring atmospheric pressure. Two types of barometer are the aneroid barometer and the mercury barometer.

BEAUFORT WIND SCALE A scale that uses observations of the effects of wind to estimate its speed.

BROKEN CLOUD Used to describe an amount of cloud covering the sky of between five and seven Oktas (eighths).

BUOYANCY In meteorology, it is the vertical force acting upon an air parcel as a result of a difference in density between the air parcel and its surrounding environment.

BUYS BALLOT'S LAW Describes the relationship of the wind direction to the pressure distribution. In the southern hemisphere, if one stands with one's back to the wind, lower pressure is to the right. Lower pressure will be to the left in the northern hemisphere.

CELSIUS TEMPERATURE SCALE (°C) A temperature scale, named after the Swedish astronomer Anders Celsius, where water at the standard sea level pressure of 1013.25 hPa has a freezing point of 0°C and a boiling point of 100°C.

CHANGE Signified by a transition between two airmasses over a relatively short time period, usually when a cooler air mass replaces a warmer airmass over an area. A change may or may not be accompanied by rain, and is characterised by a rapid change in wind direction usually from warm north to north-westerly to cooler south-east to south-westerly. A change differs from a sea breeze in that it is most often associated with the passage of a front or low pressure trough and affects a large area over a period of a day or more, as distinct from a sea breeze, which characteristically only affects areas up to around 60 km inland from the coast for a period of hours.

CHANGE OF STATE A change in the form of water, for example, liquid to vapour, ice to liquid, ice to vapour.

CIRROCUMULUS A principal cloud type, forming in the high levels of the troposphere, composed of ice crystals which appear from the ground as very small elements in the form of grains or small ripples.

CIRROSTRATUS A principal cloud type, forming in the high levels of the troposphere, composed of ice crystals which appear from the ground as a transparent sheet or veil, often creating a halo phenomenon around the sun or moon.

CIRRUS A principal cloud type, forming in the high levels of the troposphere, composed of ice crystals which appear from the ground as white tufts or filaments.

COLD FRONT The leading edge of an advancing cold air mass that is replacing warmer air.

CONDENSATION Change of state from vapour to liquid.

CONDENSATION NUCLEI Tiny particles upon which water vapour condenses.

CONDENSATION LEVEL The height at which an adiabatically lifted air parcel will become saturated, whereupon condensation occurs. Corresponds to cloud base level.

CONDITIONAL INSTABILITY Stable unsaturated air that will become unstable if saturated.

CONDUCTION The transfer of heat in response to a temperature gradient within an object or between objects that are in physical contact with one another. Transfer is from warmer to colder regions.

CONSTANT PRESSURE CHART A weather chart representing conditions on a constant pressure surface, for example, 500 hPa.

CONTACT COOLING The process whereby heat is conducted away from warmer air to a colder surface.

CONTINENTAL AIR MASS An extensive body of air, with a more or less uniform temperature and moisture profile, which has originated over a large land mass.

CONTOUR A line joining points of equal value on a surface.

CONVECTION In meteorology, it is the vertical transport of heat and moisture, especially by updrafts and downdrafts in an unstable atmosphere.

CONVECTIVE CLOUD A cloud that owes its vertical development, and possibly its origination, to convection.

CONVECTIVE CONDENSATION LEVEL The lowest height at which condensation will occur as a result of convection due to surface heating.

CONVERGENCE The condition that exists as a result of a net horizontal inflow of air into a region. Convergent winds at lower levels are associated with upward motion.

COORDINATED UNIVERSAL TIME (UTC) The primary time standard by which the world regulates clocks and time.

CORIOLIS FORCE (EFFECT) An apparent force on a moving particle that arises solely from the Earth's rotation acting as a deflecting force. It acts to the left in the southern hemisphere and to the right in the northern hemisphere. It is greatest at the poles and non-existent at the equator.

CUMULONIMBUS A principal cloud type, with bases forming in the low levels of the troposphere, characterised by a large vertical extent, and often capped by an anvil-shaped Cirrus cloud. It is often accompanied by rain showers, turbulence, icing and gusty surface winds; and sometimes also by lightning, thunder, hail, microbursts and/or tornados.

CUMULUS A principal cloud type, forming in the low levels of the troposphere, characterised by flat bases and dome or cauliflower-shaped upper surfaces. Small, separate cumulus are associated with fair-weather, but may grow into Towering Cumulus or Cumulonimbus.

DENSITY The weight of air per unit volume.

DENSITY ALTITUDE The altitude in the International Standard Atmosphere at which a given air density is found.

DEPOSITION A process in which a gas transforms into a solid, for example, the process by which water vapour, in subfreezing air, changes directly to ice without first becoming a liquid.

DEW Water in the form of small liquid drops that form on grass and other objects near the ground when the air temperature falls below its dew point, usually overnight.

DEW POINT The temperature to which air must be cooled, at constant pressure and water vapour content, in order for saturation to occur. If the air is cooled further, some of the water vapour will condense to liquid.

DIURNAL Pertaining to actions that are completed within twenty-four-hours, and recur every twenty-four hours.

DIVERGENCE Horizontal outflow of air from a particular region. Divergence at lower levels is associated with a downward movement of air.

DOLDRUMS A nautical term for the equatorial trough, an area which typically has calm or light and variable winds.

DOWNBURST A severe localised downdraft of wind from a Cumulonimbus or Towering Cumulus cloud. The outward burst of air creates damaging winds at or near the Earth's surface. The term microburst is used to describe a downburst which causes damage over an area with horizontal dimensions of less than four kilometres.

DOWNDRAFT A descent of cool air associated with convective cloud.

DOWNSLOPE WIND A wind directed down a slope, often used to describe winds produced by processes larger in scale than the slope.

DRIZZLE Slow-falling and uniformly distributed precipitation in the form of tiny water droplets (diameters less than 0.5 millimetres), usually from Stratus or Stratocumulus clouds.

DRY LINE The boundary between dry and moist air masses.

DUST Small particles of Earth or other matter suspended in the air.

EDDY A small disturbance in the wind that can produce turbulence.

ELEVATION The distance between mean sea level and a point on the Earth's surface.

EQUATOR The geographic circle at 0° latitude on the Earth's surface.

EQUILIBRIUM LEVEL The height at which a rising parcel of air will become equal in temperature to that of the environment, at which point it is no longer buoyant and thus will cease to rise in the atmosphere without forcing.

EQUATORIAL TROUGH The quasicontinuous area of low pressure located between the subtropical high pressure belts of the northern and southern hemispheres, and moving north and south with the seasons.

EVAPORATION The physical process by which a liquid, such as water, is transformed into its gaseous state.

EYE An area of clear skies that develops in the centre of a tropical cyclone. It is characterised by light winds and no rainfall.

EYE WALL An organised band of Cumulonimbus clouds that surrounds the eye of a tropical cyclone.

FAHRENHEIT TEMPERATURE SCALE (°F) The temperature scale, developed by the German physicist Daniel Gabriel Fahrenheit in 1714, where water at the standard sea level pressure of 1013.25 hPa has a freezing point of +32°F and a boiling point of +212°F.

FEEDER BANDS The lines or bands of Cumulonimbus clouds that spiral into and around the centre of a tropical cyclone.

FOG A suspension in the air, at or near the Earth's surface, of microscopic water droplets, or wet hygroscopic particles, reducing horizontal visibility to less than 1,000 metres.

FREEZING POINT The temperature at which a liquid solidifies under any given set of conditions. Pure water under the standard sea level pressure of 1013.25 hPa freezes at 0°C (32°F).

PRECIPITATION Any form of supercooled precipitation that freezes upon impact with surfaces to form glaze.

FRICTION The mechanical resistive force offered by one medium or body to the relative motion of another medium or body in contact with the first. In meteorology, it is the drag or resistance of the Earth on the atmosphere.

FRONT The transition zone or interface between two air masses of different densities.

FRONTAL PASSAGE The passage of a front over a specific point on the Earth's surface. Changes in temperature, dew point, wind, and atmospheric pressure occur with a frontal passage.

FUNNEL CLOUD A violent, rotating column of air visibly extending towards the Earth's surface from the base of a Towering Cumulus or Cumulonimbus cloud. A funnel cloud reaching the ground is called a tornado if over land, and a waterspout if over water.

GEOSTROPHIC WIND A wind that blows parallel to straight isobars above the friction layer, wherein the Coriolis force exactly balances the horizontal pressure gradient force.

GREENWICH MEAN TIME (GMT). Was used to refer to the primary time standard, but now replaced by Coordinated Universal Time (UTC).

GUST A sudden and brief increase in wind speed.

GUST FRONT The leading edge of cool air rushing down and out from a thunderstorm cloud. Is usually accompanied by a drop in temperature, a wind shift and a pressure jump, hail. Precipitation that originates in convective clouds, such as Cumulonimbus, in the form of balls or irregular pieces of ice.

HAZE A state of atmospheric obscurity due to the suspension in the air of extremely small dry particles invisible to the naked eye. Haze resembles a uniform veil over the landscape that subdues its colours. When viewed against a dark background (e.g. a mountain) it has a bluish tinge but it has a dirty yellow or orange tinge against a bright background (e.g. sun, clouds). Haze is distinguished from mist when the humidity is less than 90% at the time.

HIGH PRESSURE SYSTEM An area of pressure maximum with diverging and anticlockwise winds in the southern hemisphere and clockwise in the northern hemisphere.

INSTABILITY A state of the atmosphere where an air parcel lifted vertically will freely accelerate upward once the lifting mechanism ceases. The air parcel will form cumulus-type clouds if sufficient moisture is present.

INTERTROPICAL CONVERGENCE ZONE (ITCZ) The region where southeast and northeast trade winds meet, usually located between 10 degrees north and south of the equator. It is a broad area of low pressure, located in the southern hemisphere during our summer, and in the northern hemisphere during its summer. (Or ITZC Intertropical Zone of Convergence).

INVERSION An increase in temperature with increasing altitude, which is opposite to the usual decrease of temperature with increasing altitude.

ISOBAR A line on a chart connecting points of equal pressure.

ISOTACH A line on a chart connecting points of equal wind speed.

ISOTHERM A line on a chart connecting points of equal temperature.

KATABATIC WIND A drainage wind generated by air being cooled by conduction along a slope. The cooled air flows downhill as a katabatic wind.

KNOT A unit of speed equivalent to 1.852 kilometres per hour.

LANE BREEZE A diurnal coastal or lake breeze that blows offshore. It is caused by the temperature differences between a water surface and adjacent land.

LAPSE RATE The rate of change of temperature with height in the atmosphere.

LATENT HEAT The energy absorbed or released during a change of state. Evaporation, melting and sublimation (a change from solid to gas) absorb heat from the surrounding air as energy is needed to weaken the individual hydrogen bonds between the water molecules. Condensation, freezing and deposition (gas to solid) release the latent heat, thus adding heat to the surrounding air.

LATITUDE A geographic coordinate that specifies the north–south position of a point on the Earth's surface. It is measured as the angular distance, subtended at the Earth's centre, along a meridian from a point on the Earth to the equator. The equator is designated as zero degrees and the poles as 90 degrees.

LEE (LEESIDE/LEEWARD) The side of an obstacle that is furthest away from the wind.

LEVEL OF FREE CONVECTION The height at which a parcel of saturated air becomes warmer than the surrounding air and thus begins to rise freely until it reaches its equilibrium level.

LIGHTNING A visible electrical discharge produced by a Cumulonimbus cloud. It can occur between cloud and ground, between clouds, within a single cloud, or between a cloud and surrounding air.

LONGITUDE A geographic coordinate that specifies the east–west position of a point on the Earth's surface. It is measured as an angle in reference to the Prime Meridian, which is designated as zero degrees longitude.

LOW LATITUDES The latitude belt between the equator and 30 degrees north and south of the equator.

PRESSURE SYSTEM An area of pressure minimum with converging winds rotating clockwise in the southern hemisphere and anticlockwise in the northern hemisphere.

MARITIME AIR MASS An air mass that has originated over an extensive water surface.

MEAN SEA LEVEL (MSL) The height of the sea surface, measured with respect to land-based benchmarks, after averaging out variations due to tides and waves.

MEAN SEA LEVEL PRESSURE (MSLP) The atmospheric pressure at mean sea level.

MICROBURST Used to refer to a severe downburst of wind, usually from a thunderstorm, over an area of less than four kilometres in diameter. The term downburst is used to refer to larger diameters.

MIST A suspension in the air, at or near the Earth's surface, of microscopic water droplets or wet hygroscopic particles which reduce the horizontal visibility to less than 5,000 metres but not less than 1,000 metres.

MONSOON The seasonal shift of winds caused by the much greater annual variation of temperature over large land areas compared with neighbouring ocean surfaces, which results in an excess of air pressure over the land areas in winter and a deficit in summer. The monsoon is strongest on the southern and eastern sides of Asia.

NIMBOSTRATUS low or middle-level thick dark cloud with more or less continuously falling rain, snow or sleet.

OCCLUDED FRONT A front formed when a cold front overtakes a warm front.

POLAR AIR MASS An air mass that forms over a high latitude region. Continental polar air is formed over cold land surfaces and is typically very stable with low moisture.

POLAR FRONT A semicontinuous, semipermanent boundary between polar and subtropical air masses.

PRECIPITATION Any or all of the forms of water, whether liquid (e.g. rain, drizzle) or solid (e.g. hail, snow), that fall from a cloud or group of clouds and reach the ground.

PREFRONTAL SQUALL LINE A line of thunderstorms that may develop ahead of an advancing cold front, and having an orientation more or less parallel to the cold front.

PREFRONTAL TROUGH An elongated area of relatively low pressure that may develop ahead of an advancing cold front.

PRESSURE GRADIENT The pressure change that occurs over a fixed distance.

PREVAILING WIND A wind that blows from one direction more frequently than any other during a given period.

RADAR Acronym for Radio Detection and Ranging. An electronic instrument used to detect distant objects and measure their range by detecting scattered or reflected radio energy.

RADIATION The process by which energy is propagated through any medium by virtue of the wave motion in that medium. Electromagnetic radiation, which emits heat and light, is one form.

RADIATIONAL COOLING The cooling of the Earth's surface and the adjacent air which occurs at night when the Earth's surface suffers a net loss of heat due to outgoing radiation being greater than incoming radiation.

RADIATION FOG Fog that forms when radiational cooling at the Earth's surface lowers the temperature of the air near the ground to, or below, its dew point.

RAIN Precipitation in the form of liquid water droplets greater than 0.5 mm diameter.

RELATIVE HUMIDITY The ratio of the vapour pressure to the saturation vapour pressure with respect to water. Also known as the ratio of the existing amount of water vapour to that which could be held by a parcel of air. It is usually expressed as a percentage.

RIDGE An elongated area of high pressure.

ROLL CLOUD A low-level, horizontal, tube-shaped cloud. Usually associated with a thunderstorm gust front, where the roll cloud is completely detached from the base of the Cumulonimbus cloud. It will sometimes form with a cold front.

SATURATE To add something to the point where no more can be absorbed, dissolved, or retained. In meteorology, it is used when discussing the amount of water vapour in a volume of air.

SCATTERED Used to describe an amount of cloud covering the sky of three or four oktas (eighths).

SEA BREEZE A diurnal coastal breeze that blows onshore due a temperature differential between the land and the water.

SEA BREEZE FRONT The discontinuity in temperature and humidity that marks the leading edge of the intrusion of cool and moist marine air associated with a sea breeze.

SEA FOG A type of advection fog that forms when warm moist air advects over water with a cooler temperature, and the consequent cooling of that air to below its dewpoint by the underlying cooler water. (Advect is the transfer (heat or matter) by the flow of a fluid, especially horizontally in the atmosphere or the sea).

SEVERE THUNDERSTORM The BOM defines a severe thunderstorm as one with winds of around 50 knots or greater, or hail of diameter 2 cm or larger, or tornados or flash floods.

SHOWERS Rain events that begin and end suddenly, are relatively short-lived, but may last half an hour. Showers fall from Cumulus clouds, often separated by blue sky. Showers may fall in patches rather than across the whole forecast area and range in intensity from light to very heavy.

SQUALL A sudden onset of strong winds with speeds increasing by at least 16 knots and sustained at 22 or more knots for at least one minute. On the Beaufort Scale the increase in wind is by at least three forces to a Force 6 or more. The intensity and duration are longer than that of a gust.

SQUALL LINE THUNDERSTORMS A continuous line of thunderstorms accompanied by a surface gust front at the line's leading edge.

STABLE ATMOSPHERE A state of the atmosphere in which a lifted air parcel will sink to its equilibrium level once the lifting mechanism ceases, due to the air parcel being denser (cooler) than the surrounding air.

STANDARD ATMOSPHERE A mathematical model of the atmosphere which is standardised so that predictable calculations can be made.

STANDING WAVE An atmospheric wave that is stationary with respect to the Earth's surface.

STEAM FOG Fog that forms when cool air, passing over warm water, reaches its saturation point due to water evaporating from the warm water into the cooler air. Fog rising in the convection currents above the water give rise to a steaming appearance.

STRATIFORM Clouds that exhibit extensive horizontal development (in contrast to the vertical development of cumuliform clouds).

STRATOCUMULUS A principal cloud type, forming in the low levels of the troposphere and existing in a relatively flat layer but having individual elements, from which drizzle can fall. It can form from Cumulus clouds becoming more stratified when they push up into a stable atmospheric layer.

STRATOPAUSE The boundary zone between the stratosphere and the mesosphere. In the stratosphere the temperature increases with height, with the stratopause being the point of maximum temperature, prior to a decrease in temperature in the mesosphere.

STRATOSPHERE The layer of the atmosphere located between the troposphere and the mesosphere. It is characterised by an increase in temperature with height and an absence of convective clouds and associated turbulence.

STRATUS A principal cloud type, forming in the low levels of the troposphere and normally existing as a flat layer that does not exhibit individual elements.

SUBLIMATION The process of ice changing directly into water vapour.

SUN PROTECTION TIMES The times of the day when sun protection measures are recommended such as "slip, slop, slap, seek and slide". This is when the UV Index is 3 and above in clear sky conditions.

SUPERCELL A Cumulonimbus cloud characterised by a rotating and long-lived, intense updraft. They can potentially result in the most severe thunderstorms, capable of producing extremely large hail, damaging winds and violent tornados.

SUPERCOOLING The reduction of the temperature of a liquid below its freezing point without it becoming a solid.

SYNOPTIC CHART Any chart that depicts meteorological or atmospheric conditions over a large area at a given time.

THERMOSPHERE The layer of the atmosphere located between the mesosphere and outer space. It is a region of increasing temperature with height, and includes all of the exosphere and most of the ionosphere.

THUNDER The sound emitted by rapidly expanding gases along the channel of a lightning discharge.

THUNDERSTORM A Cumulonimbus cloud characterised by thunder and lightning and associated gusty surface winds, hail, rain, turbulence, icing and, under the most severe conditions, microbursts and/or tornados.

TORNADO A tall, rapidly rotating column of air between 5 and 1,000 metres in diameter which is attached to the base of a Cumulonimbus or large Cumulus cloud and which is capable of producing damage at the Earth's surface. Tornados may form water spouts when they occur over water.

TOWERING CUMULUS A vertically developed cumulus cloud, often a precursor to Cumulonimbus.

TRADE WINDS Two belts of prevailing wind that blow easterly from the subtropical high pressure centres in each hemisphere towards the Equatorial Trough. They are characterised by their great consistency of direction. To the north of the trough they blow from the northeast, and to the south of the trough they blow from the southeast.

TROPICS The region of the Earth located between the Tropic of Cancer, at 23.5 degrees north and the Tropic of Capricorn, at 23.5 degrees south.

TROPICAL AIR MASS An air mass that forms in the tropics or subtropics. Maritime tropical air is produced over oceans and is warm and humid, while continental tropical air is formed over arid land and is very hot and dry.

TROPICAL CYCLONE A non-frontal low pressure system that develops over tropical waters. In Australia, the term severe tropical cyclone is used when winds reach or exceed 64 knots.

TROPICAL DISTURBANCE An area of organised convection, originating in the tropics or occasionally the subtropics, that maintains its identity for twenty-four-hours or more, but has no closed wind circulation. It is often the first developmental stage of a tropical cyclone.

TROPIC OF CANCER Located at 23.5 degrees north, it is the most northern point on the Earth where the sun is directly overhead (on 21 June).

TROPIC OF CAPRICORN Located at 23.5 degrees south, it is the most southern point on the Earth where the sun is directly overhead (on 22 December).

TROPOPAUSE The boundary zone or transition layer between the troposphere and the stratosphere.

TROPOSPHERE The lowest layer of the atmosphere. Is characterised by clouds, weather and a decrease in temperature with increasing altitude.

TROUGH An elongated area of low atmospheric pressure.

TURBULENCE Irregular fluctuations occurring in fluid motions.

UNSTABLE ATMOSPHERE An atmosphere in which air parcels rise buoyantly due to the rising air parcel being less dense (warmer) than the surrounding air.

UPDRAFT A small-scale current of air with marked vertical motion.

VEERING A clockwise shift in the wind direction.

VIRGA Precipitation that falls from clouds but evaporates before reaching the ground.

VISIBILITY A measure of the opacity of the atmosphere. It is the greatest distance one can see prominent objects with unaided normal eyesight.

WARM FRONT The leading edge of an advancing warm air mass that is replacing a relatively colder air mass.

WATER VAPOUR Water in its gaseous form.

WAVE HEIGHT The vertical distance between the top of crest and bottom of trough.

WAVE HEIGHT (KING/FREAK) These waves can occur when wind waves and/or a combination of swell waves join to produce a very high wave. These can be even higher than the probable maximum wave height, and can result from the added influence of currents, tides, distant weather systems and shape and depth of the seabed.

WAVE HEIGHT (TOTAL) The height is the combination of wind waves and swell.

WAVE HEIGHT (SIGNIFICANT) The wave and swell heights described in BOM observations and forecasts refer to "significant wave heights" which represent the average of the highest one-third of the waves. Some waves will be higher and some lower than the significant wave height. The probable maximum wave height can be up to twice the significant wave height.

WAVES (SWELL) The regular longer period waves that were generated by the winds of distant weather systems. There may be several sets of swell waves travelling in different directions, causing a confused seas state.

WAVE LENGTH The distance between two successive wave crests separated by a trough.

WIND DIRECTION The direction from which the wind is blowing.

WIND SHEAR A wind direction and/or speed change over a vertical or horizontal distance.

WIND SPEED Wind speed mentioned in forecasts and coastal observations refers to the average speed over a 10-minute period at a height of 10 metres above the surface. It is given in knots. A knot (kn) is equal to a speed of one nautical mile per hour. Note: 10 knots = 18.5 km/h and 10 km/h = 5.4 knots.

WIND (OR SEA) WAVES Generated by the local prevailing wind and vary in size according to the length of time a particular wind has been blowing, the fetch (distance the wind has blown over the sea) and the water depth.

WINDY A prolonged period of average wind speeds exceeding 40km/h during the day.

Why Choose Us

Our philosophy
"There is no such thing as a silly question"
and
"Be an encourager there are far too many critics in the world already".

With over **60** years combined, international experience, we will share all our experience with you, gained from traversing over 80,000 nautical miles.

- Trained local NSW Marine Police
- Taught commercial maritime tickets at TAFE
- Ex-Marine Rescue Skippers
- Circumnavigated the world one-and-a-half times (we've circumnavigated Tahiti too!)
- Award winning Skippers (joint top student Master 5, top student MED3)
- Award winning authors
- Written pilot books
- Written best-selling memoirs (on our travels)
- Written manuals on: Navigation, Weather, and created a useful Log Book (Shop Nautical)
- Host a popular Podcast Show: Turning your Cruising Dreams into Reality
- Professional maritime trainers for 10 years
- Taught/sailed/worked on a variety of boats all over the world
- Utilised a wide variety of marine equipment (VHF/HF/MF, Navigation systems, radar)
- AIS, GPS, plotters, Weather, etc), all over the world
- Partnered with a Registered Training Organisation and we conform to National Training Standards
- Everyone is treated equally and fairly
- Documented safety system – we look after your personal details
- Competitive pricing

We love all things boating, and we are super proud to watch many of our students turn into great skippers!
One of our team has even set a blue-water sailing record!

Don't take our word for it, read the testimonials on our website
www.sistershiptraining.com

In Partnership with RTO 20665 – The Learning Professionals – ABN 87 281 145 065

SHOP NAUTICAL
WWW.SISTERSHIPTRAINING.COM

BY THE SAME AUTHOR, AVAILABLE FROM: WWW.SISTERSHIPTRAINING.COM/SHOPNAUTICAL

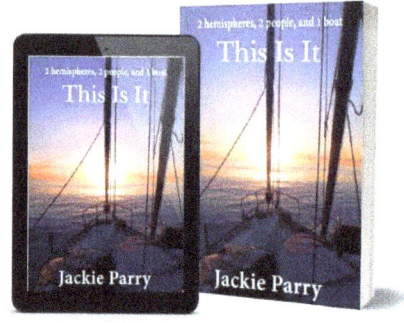

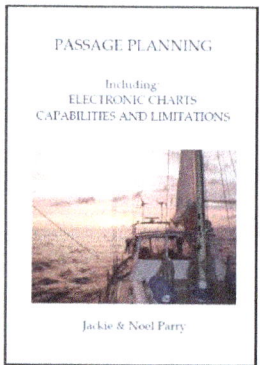
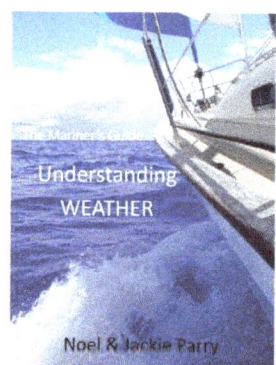

www.ingramcontent.com/pod-product-compliance
Lightning Source LLC
Chambersburg PA
CBHW040315240426
43663CB00025B/2976